Classical Guitar Tunes

JIGS & REELS

I0803028

by Ed Munger

Online Audio

To access the online audio go to:
WWW.MELBAY.COM/30895MEB

WWW.MELBAY.COM

Table of Contents

Title	Page	Audio
The Girl I Left Behind	3	1
Comin' Through The Rye	4	2
The Waterman	5	3
Come Haste To The Wedding	6	4
Paddy O'Rafferty	7	5
St. Patrick's Day	8	6
White Cockade	9	7
Wait For The Wagon	10	8
Rory O'More	11	9
Camptown Hornpipe	12	10
Basket Figure	13	11
Land of Sweet Erin	14	12
Durang's Hornpipe	15	13
Fisher's Hornpipe	16	14
Scottish Hornpipe	17	15
Highland Fling	18	16
Roy's Wife of Aldrivalloch (Highland Reel)	19	17
Rosa Lee	20	18
Original Banjo Dance	22	19
Kinlock	23	20
Speed the Plough	24	21
Miss McLeod's Reel	25	22
Martha	26	23
Virginia (Lord MacDonald's Reel)	28	24
The Highland Lassie	30	25
Farewell Bonnie Scotland	32	26
Chorus Jig	34	27
The Campbells Are Comin'	35	28
There's Nae Luck About The House	37	29
My Love She's But A Lassie Yet	38	30
About the Author	40	

Acknowledgments

I would like to thank my Father, Edgar W. Munger, for all the support he gave me.
Also: Tim Lynch at Center Stage Studios.

The Girl I Left Behind

Traditional
(arranged for guitar by Ed Munger)

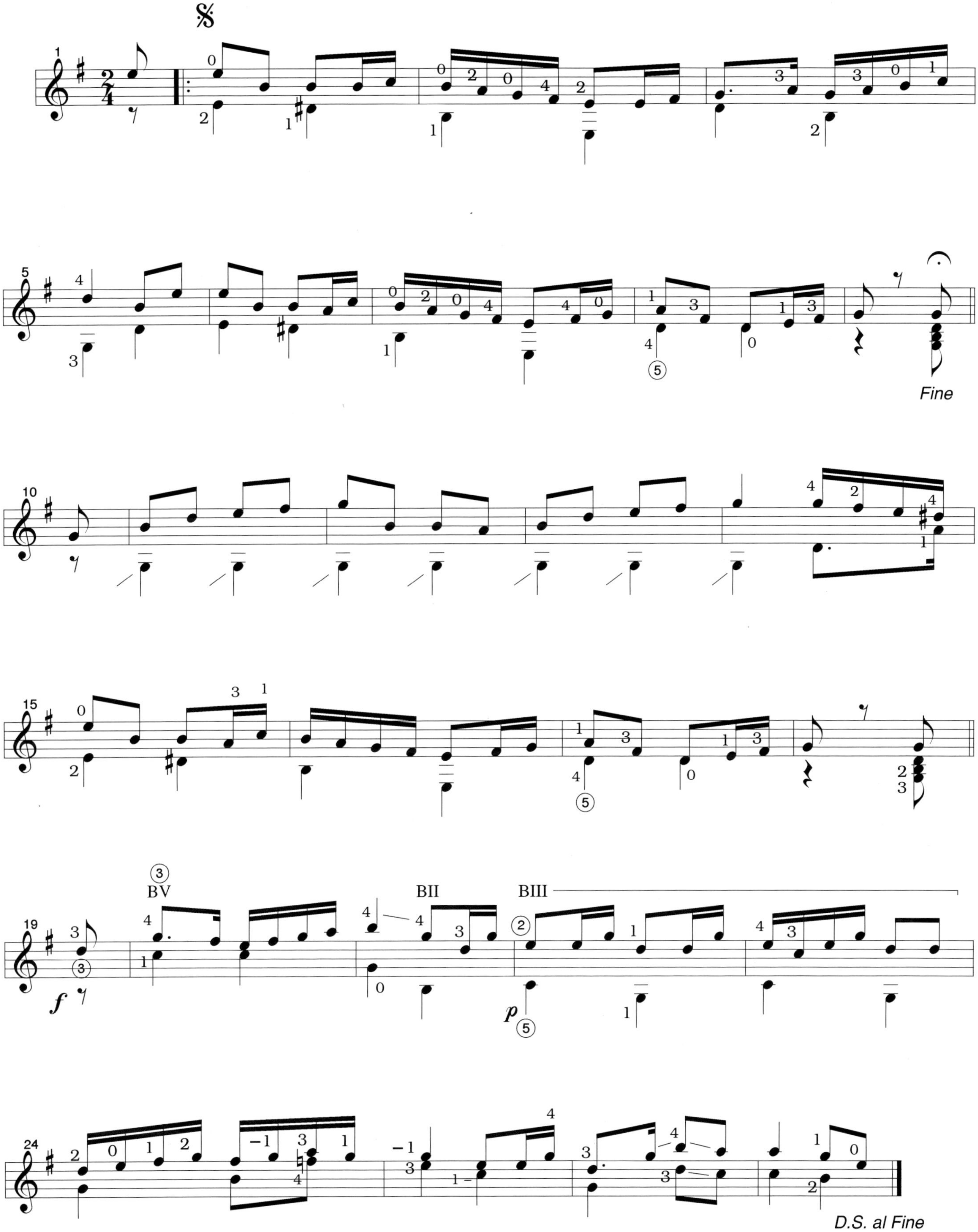

Comin' Thro' the Rye

Traditional
(arranged for guitar by Ed Munger)

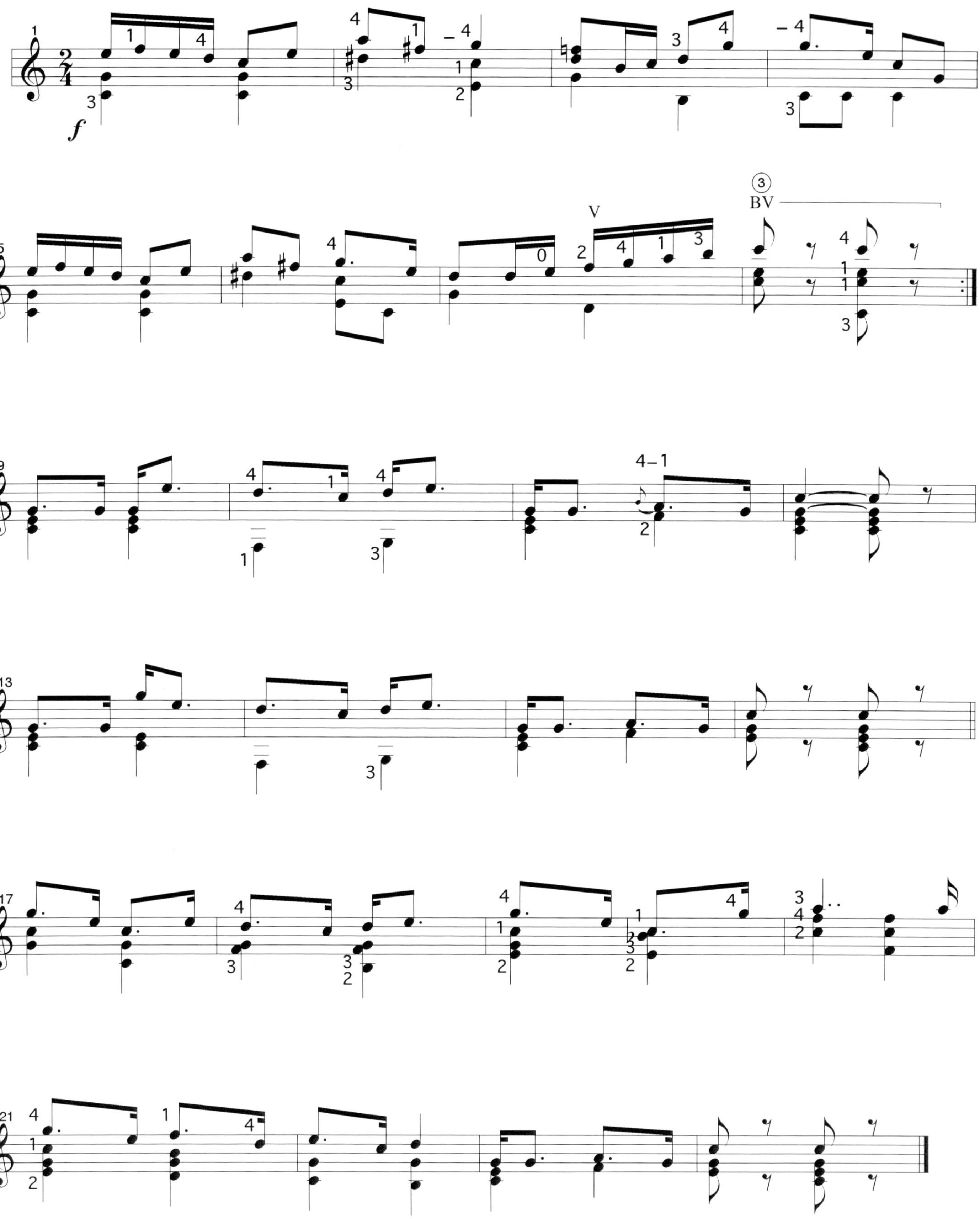

The Waterman

Traditional
(arranged for guitar by Ed Munger)

6th = D
5th = G

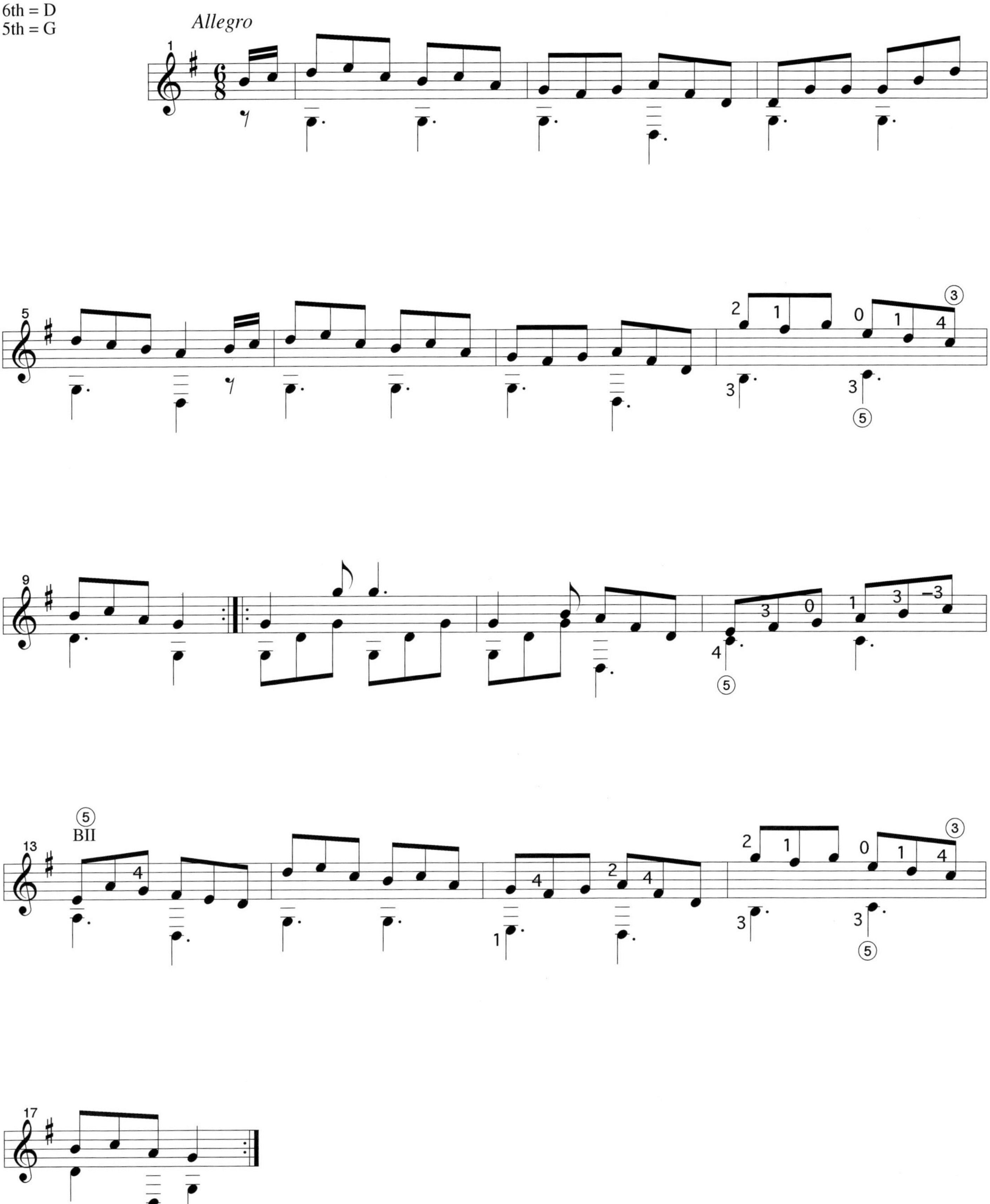

Come Haste to the Wedding

Traditional
(arranged for guitar by Ed Munger)

6th = D

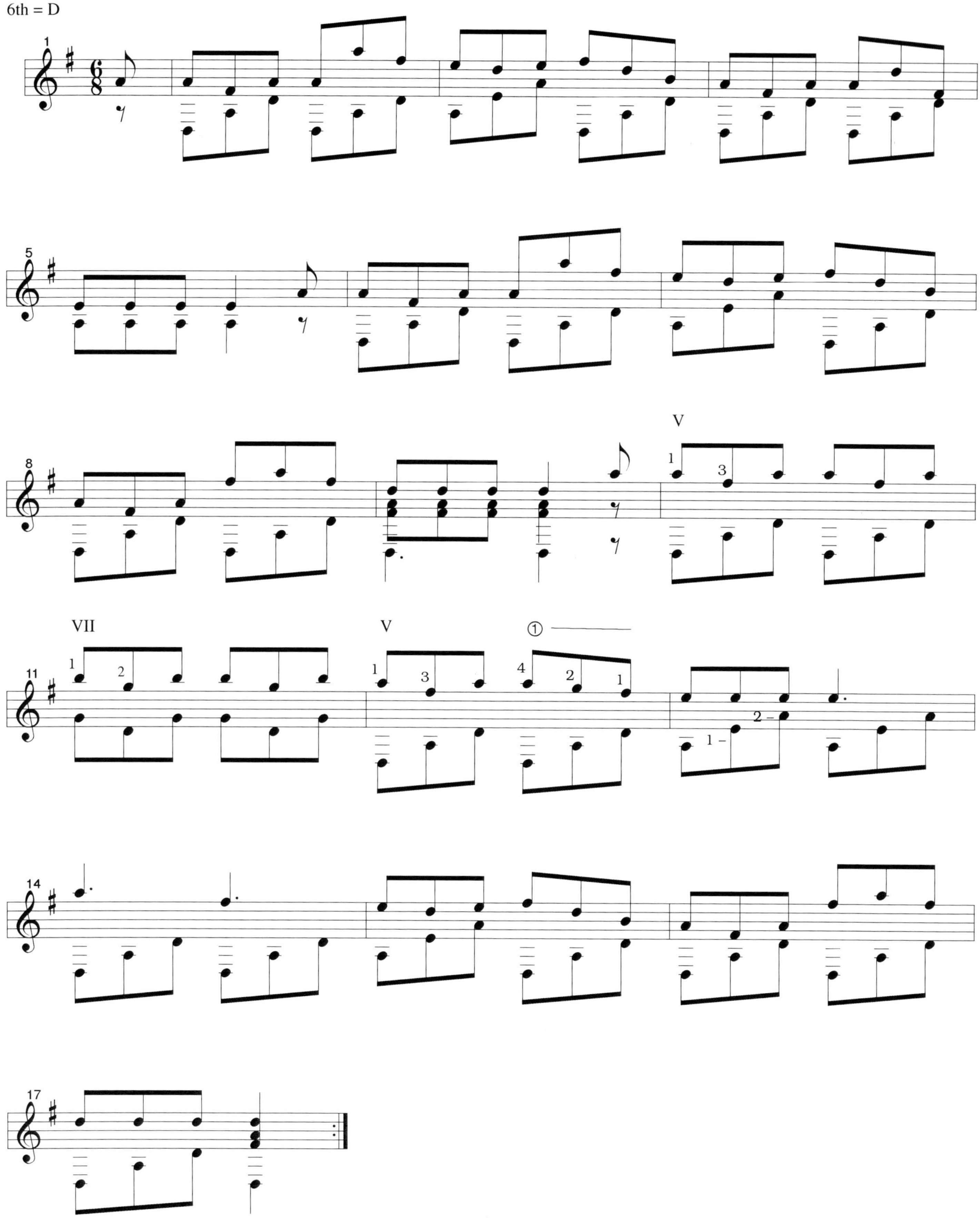

Paddy O'Rafferty

Traditional
(arranged for guitar by Ed Munger)

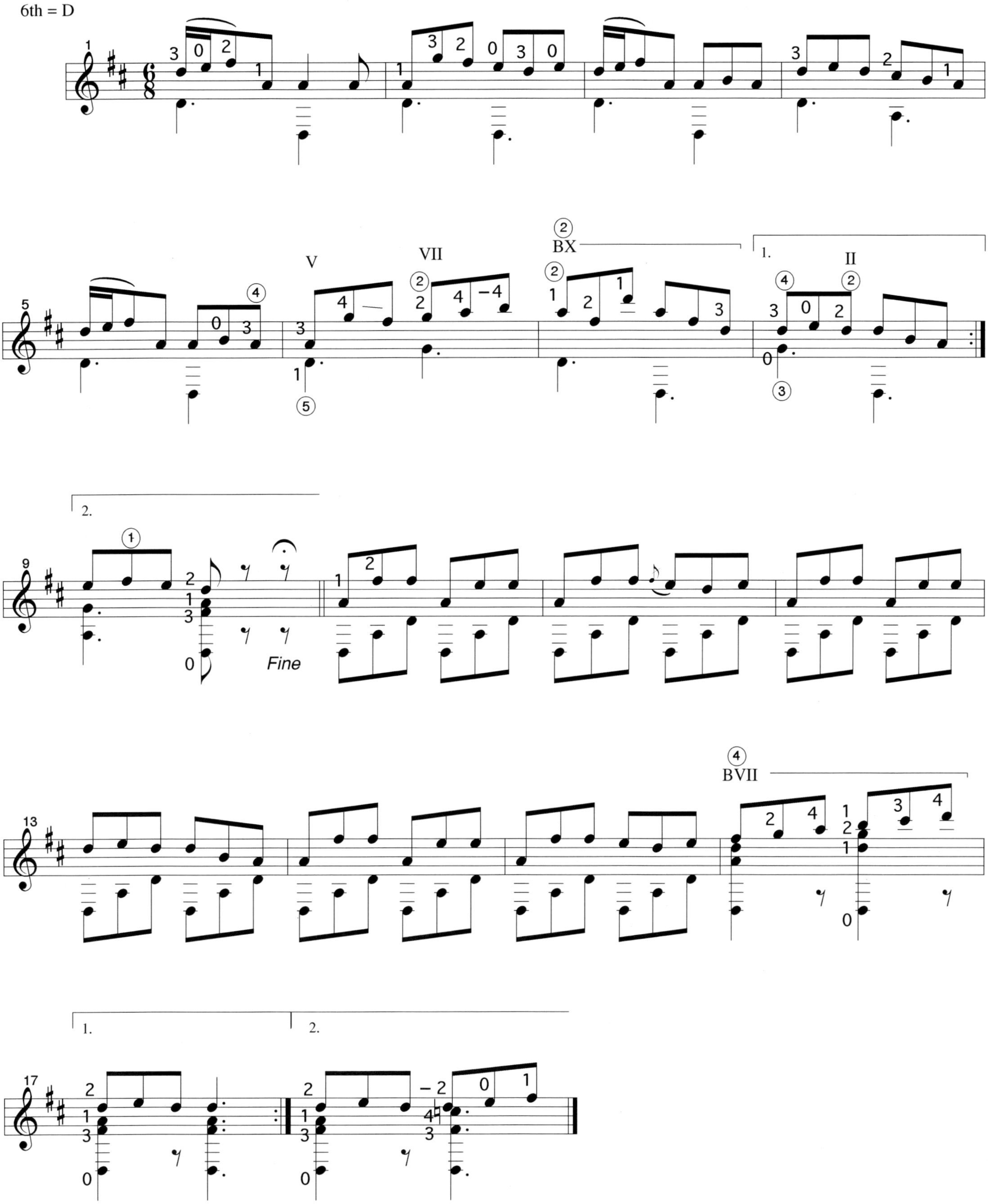

St. Patricks Day

(continue from Paddy O'Rafferty)

Traditional
(arranged for guitar by Ed Munger)

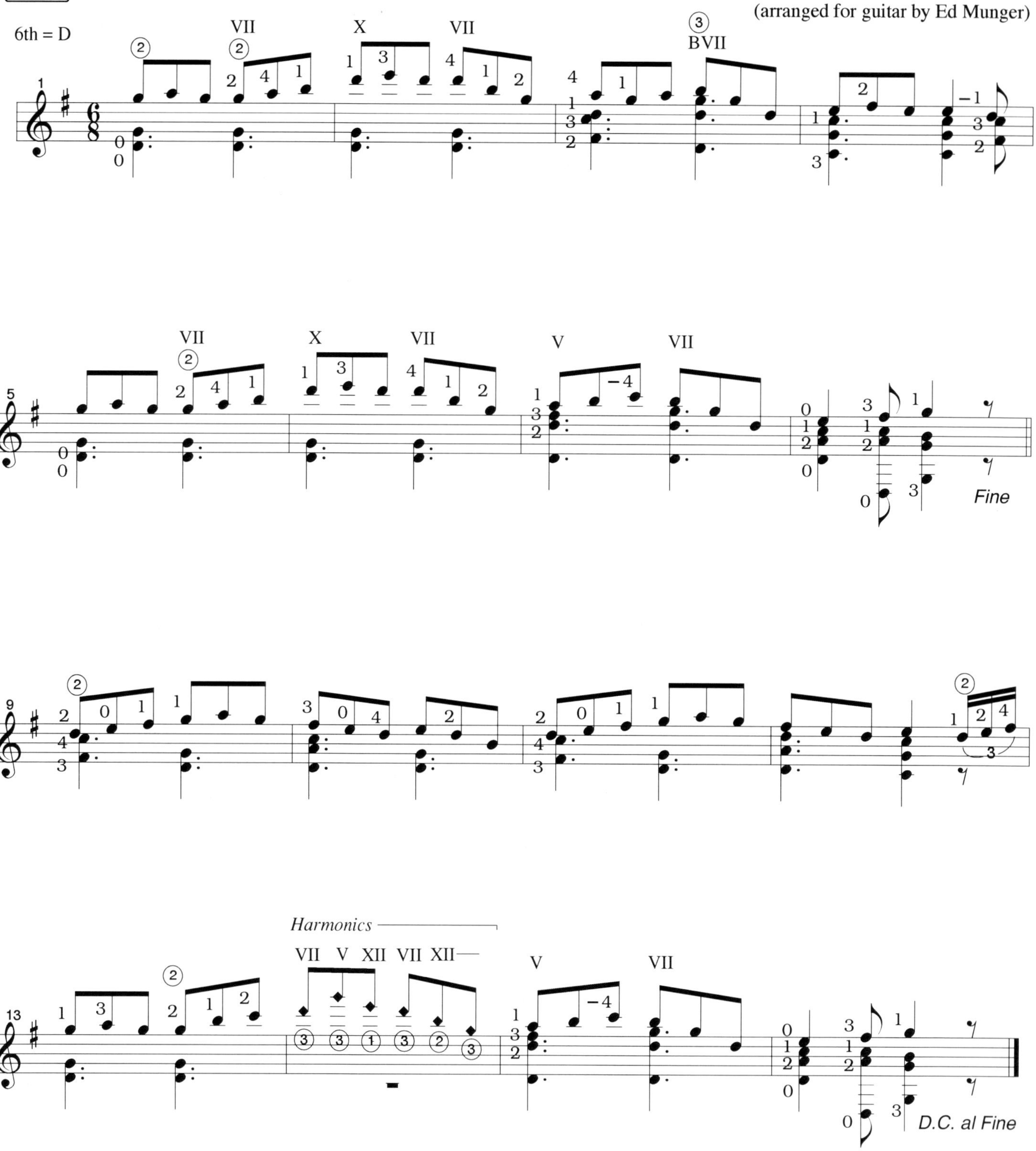

7

White Cockade

Traditional
(arranged for guitar by Ed Munger)

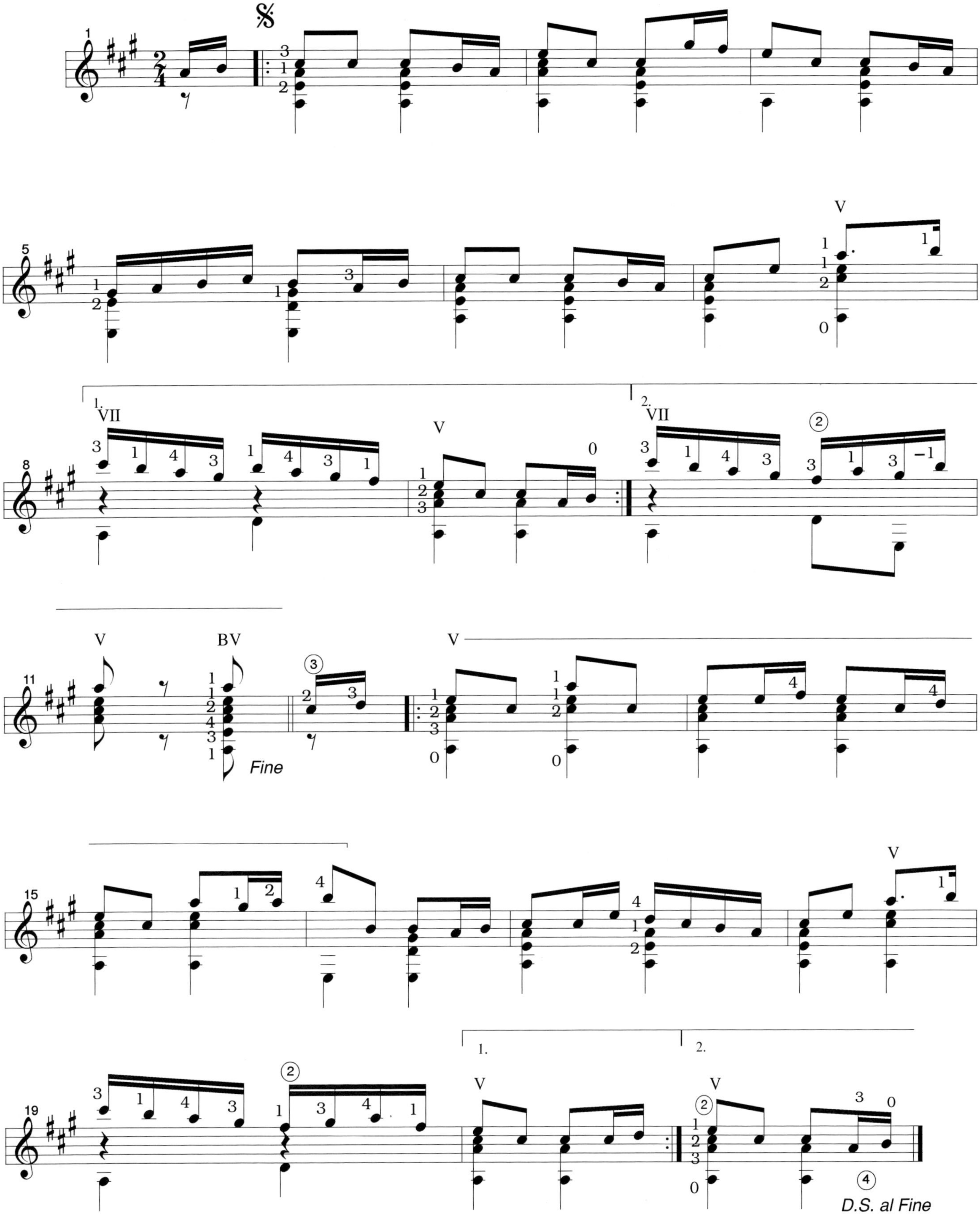

8

Wait For The Wagon

Traditional
(arranged for guitar by Ed Munger)

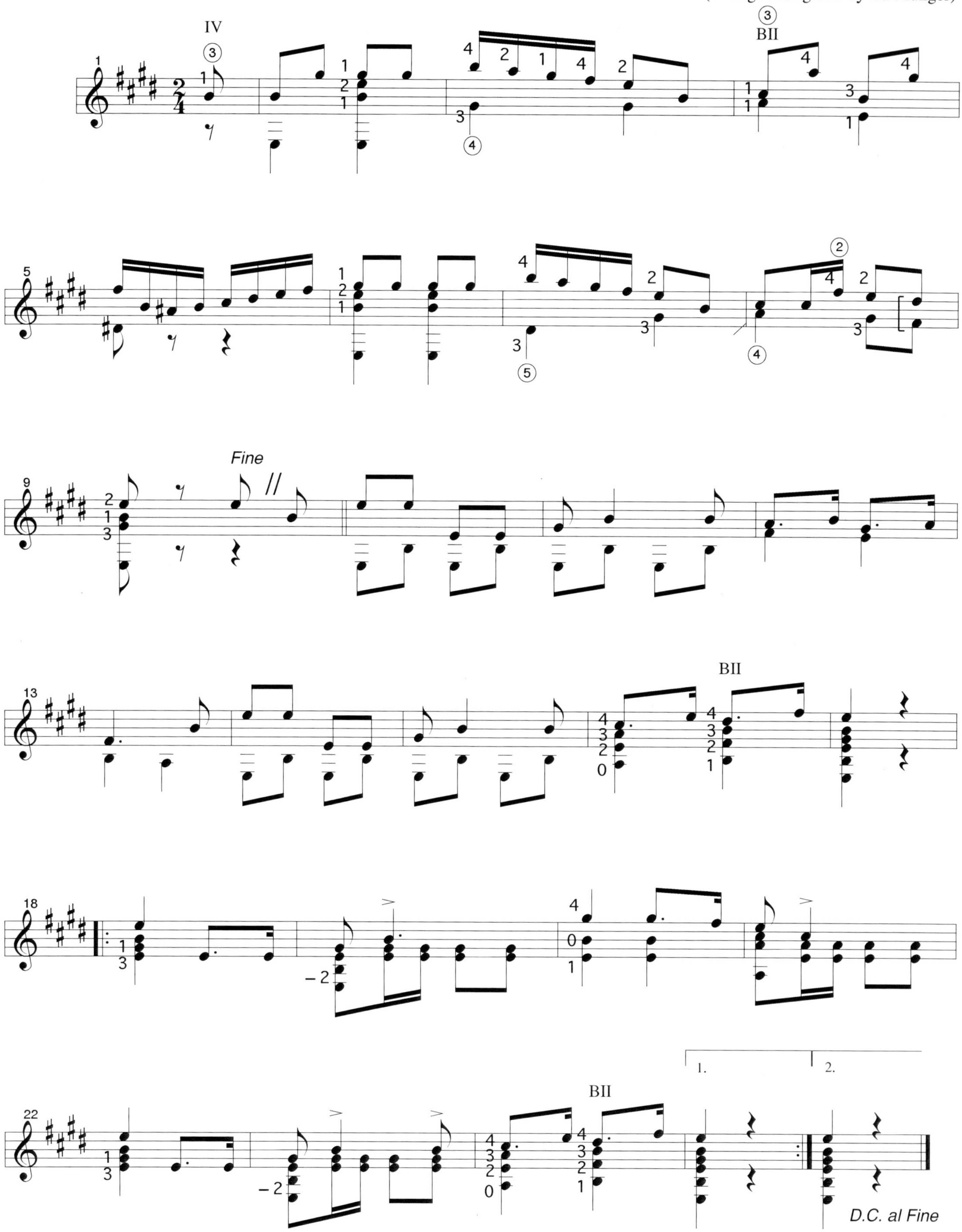

9

Rory O'More

Traditional
(arranged for guitar by Ed Munger)

6th = D
5th = G

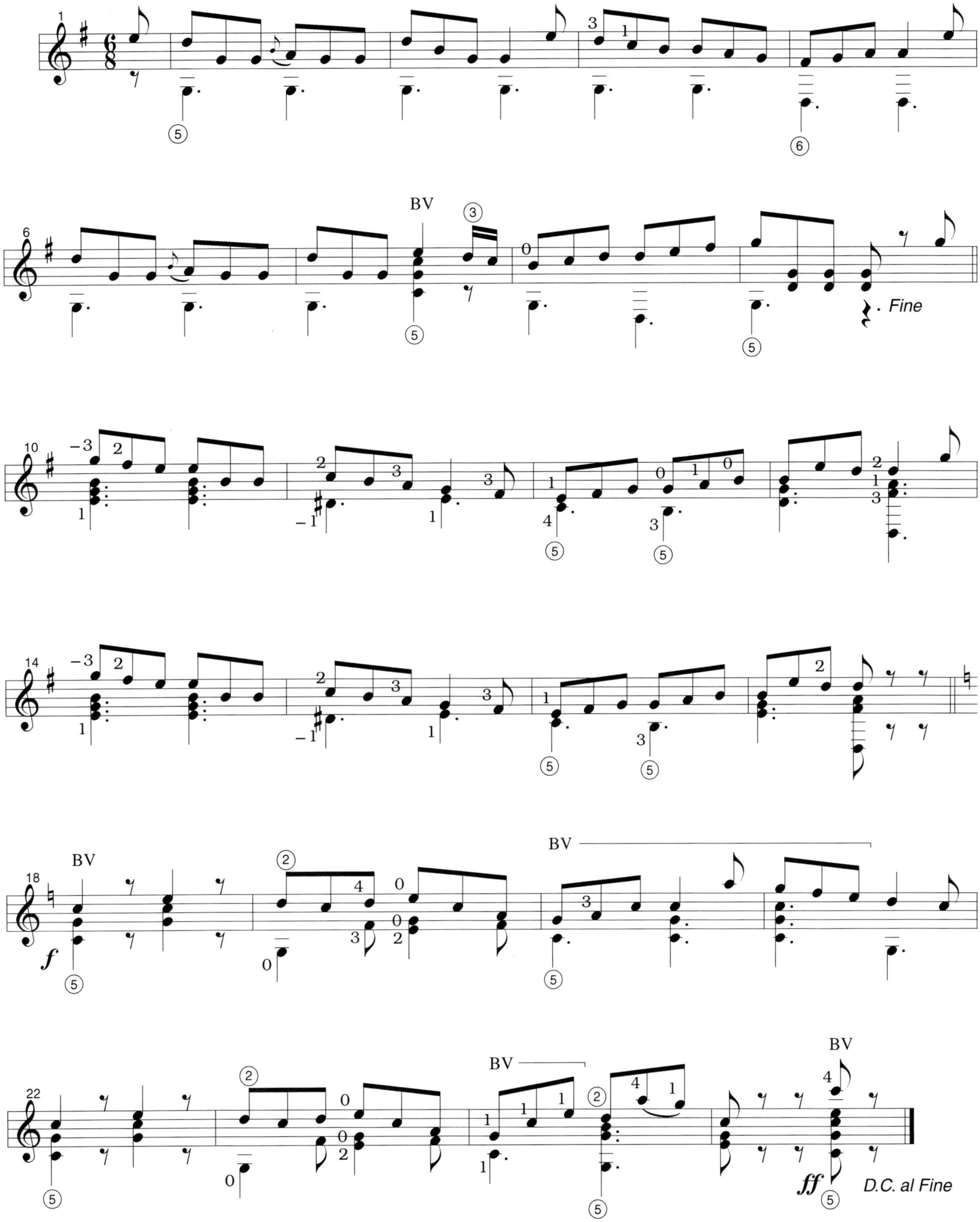

10

Camptown Hornpipe

Traditional
(arranged for guitar by Ed Munger)

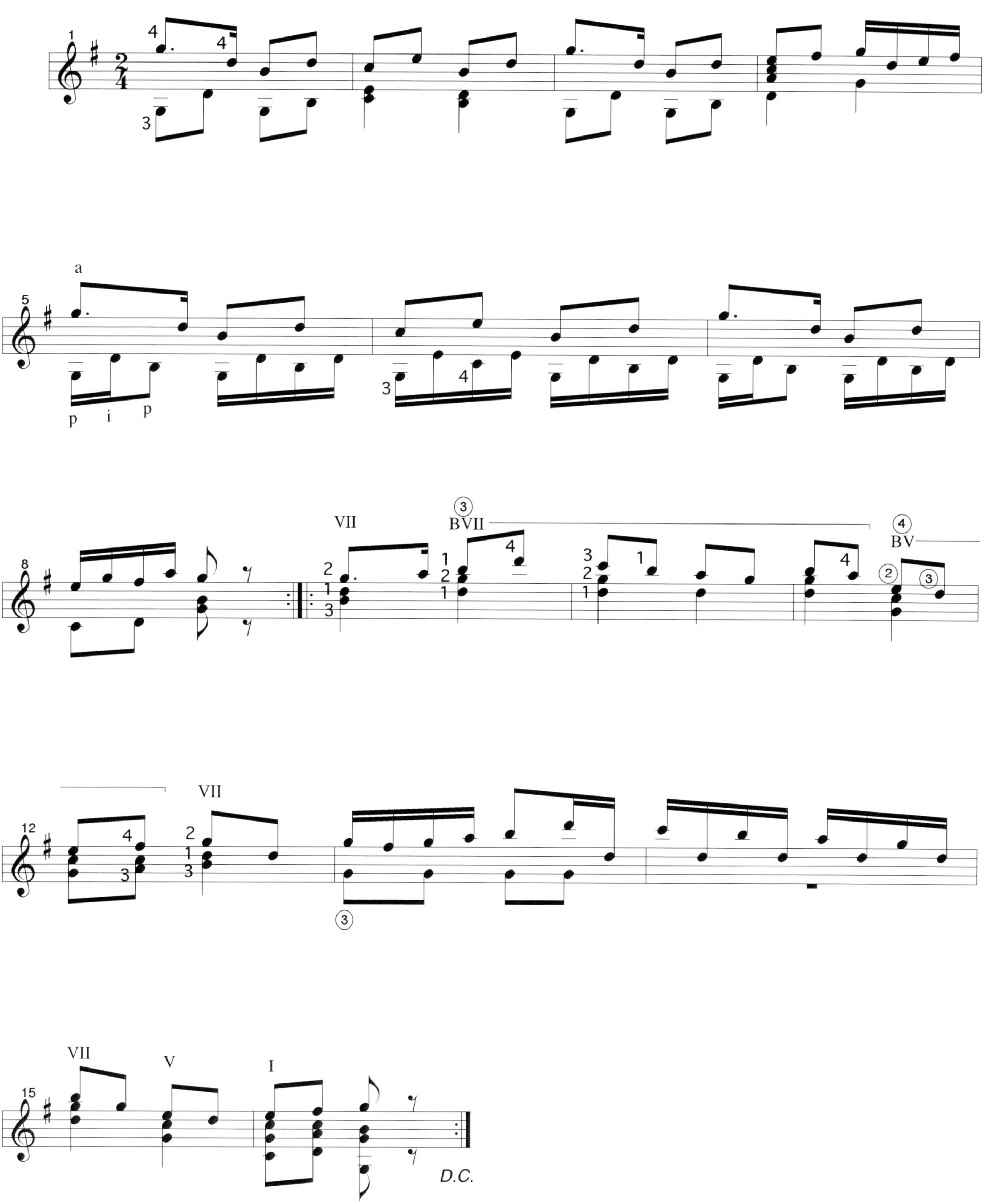

Basket Figure

Malbrook
(arranged for guitar by Ed Munger)

6th = D

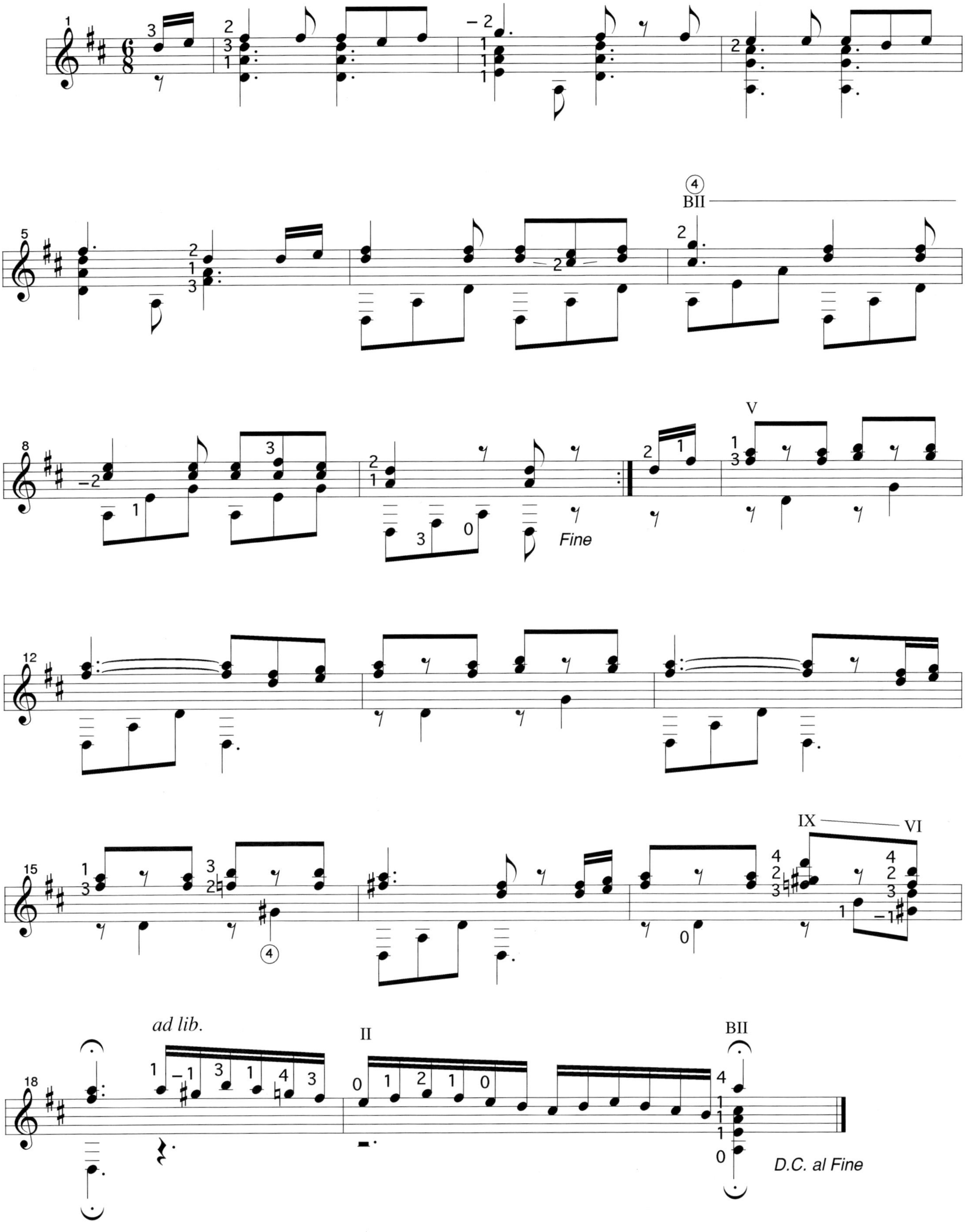

12

Land of Sweet Erin

Malbrook
(arranged for guitar by Ed Munger)

6th = D
5th = G

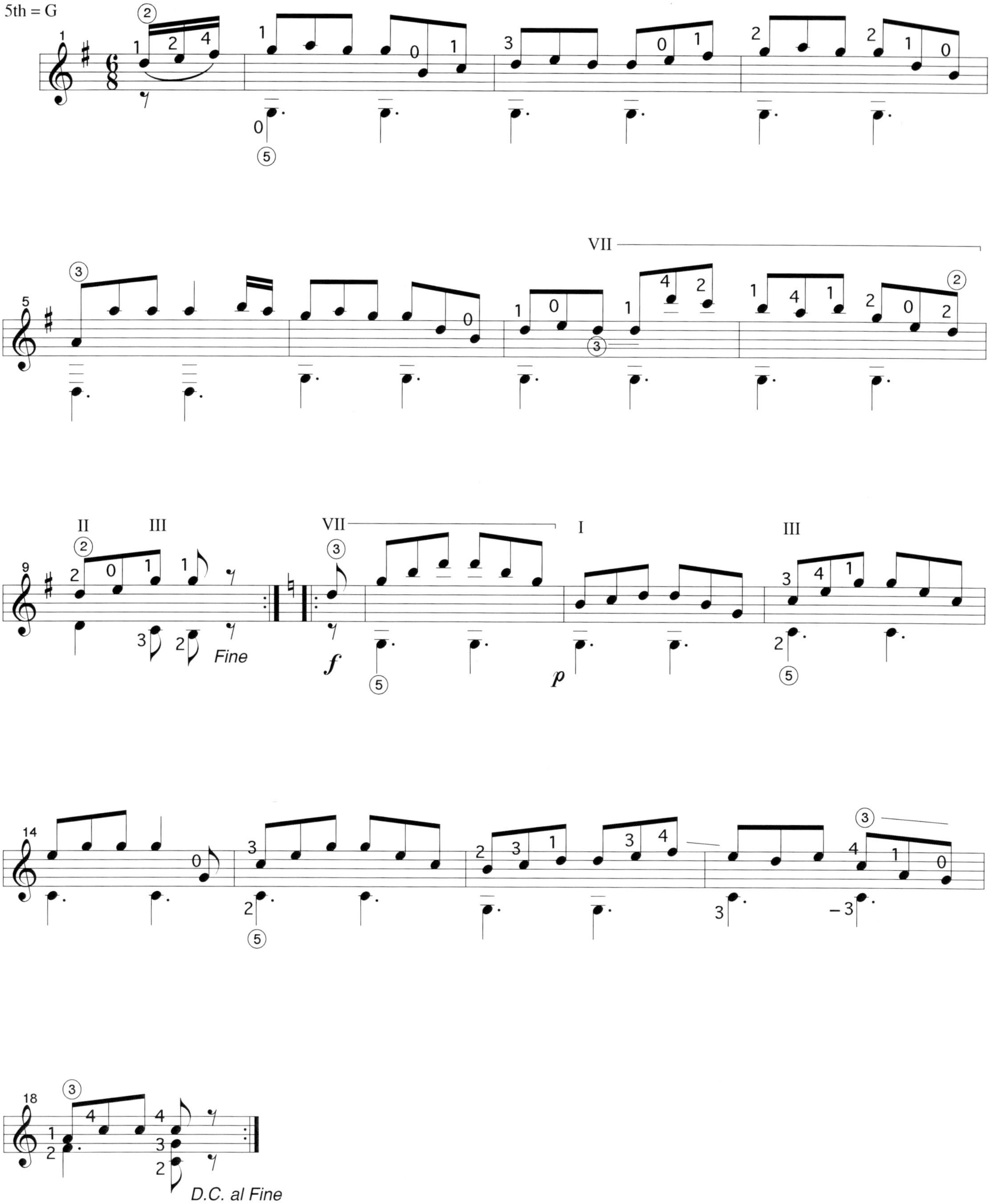

13

Durang's Hornpipe

Traditional
(arranged for guitar by Ed Munger)

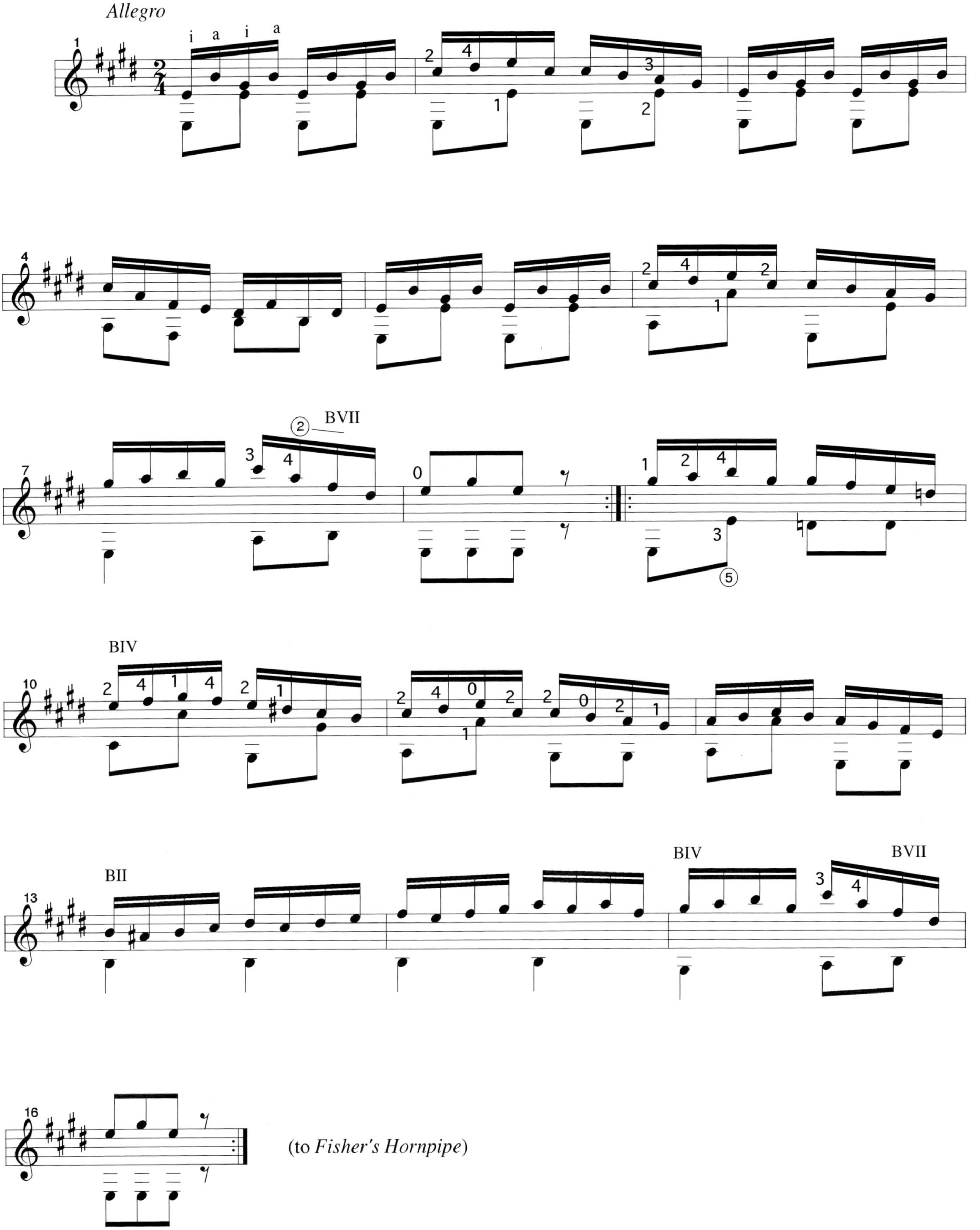

14

Fisher's Hornpipe

(continue from *Durang's Hornpipe*)

Traditional
(arranged for guitar by Ed Munger)

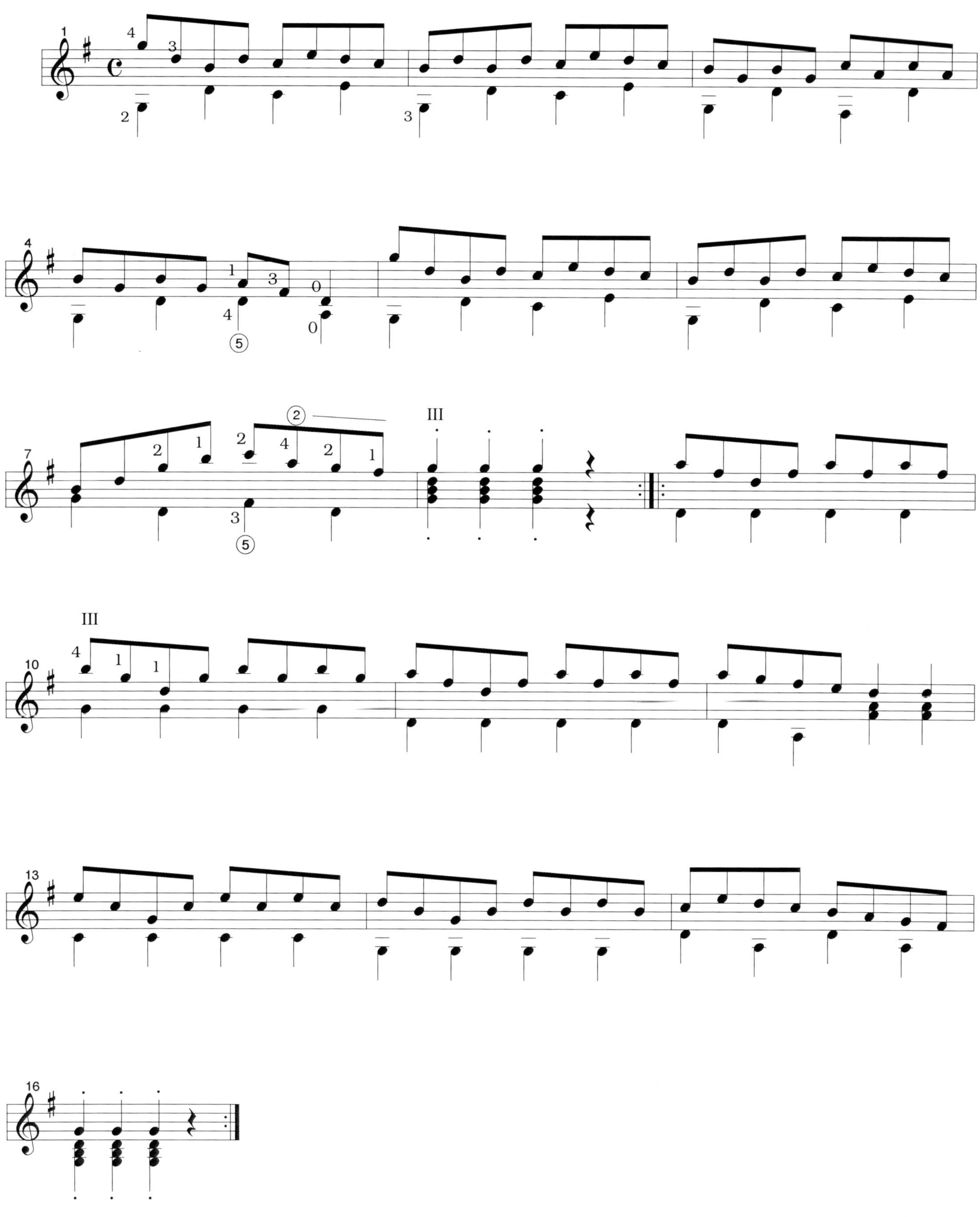

Scottish Hornpipe

W.K. Batchelder
(arranged for guitar by Ed Munger)

(original in G)

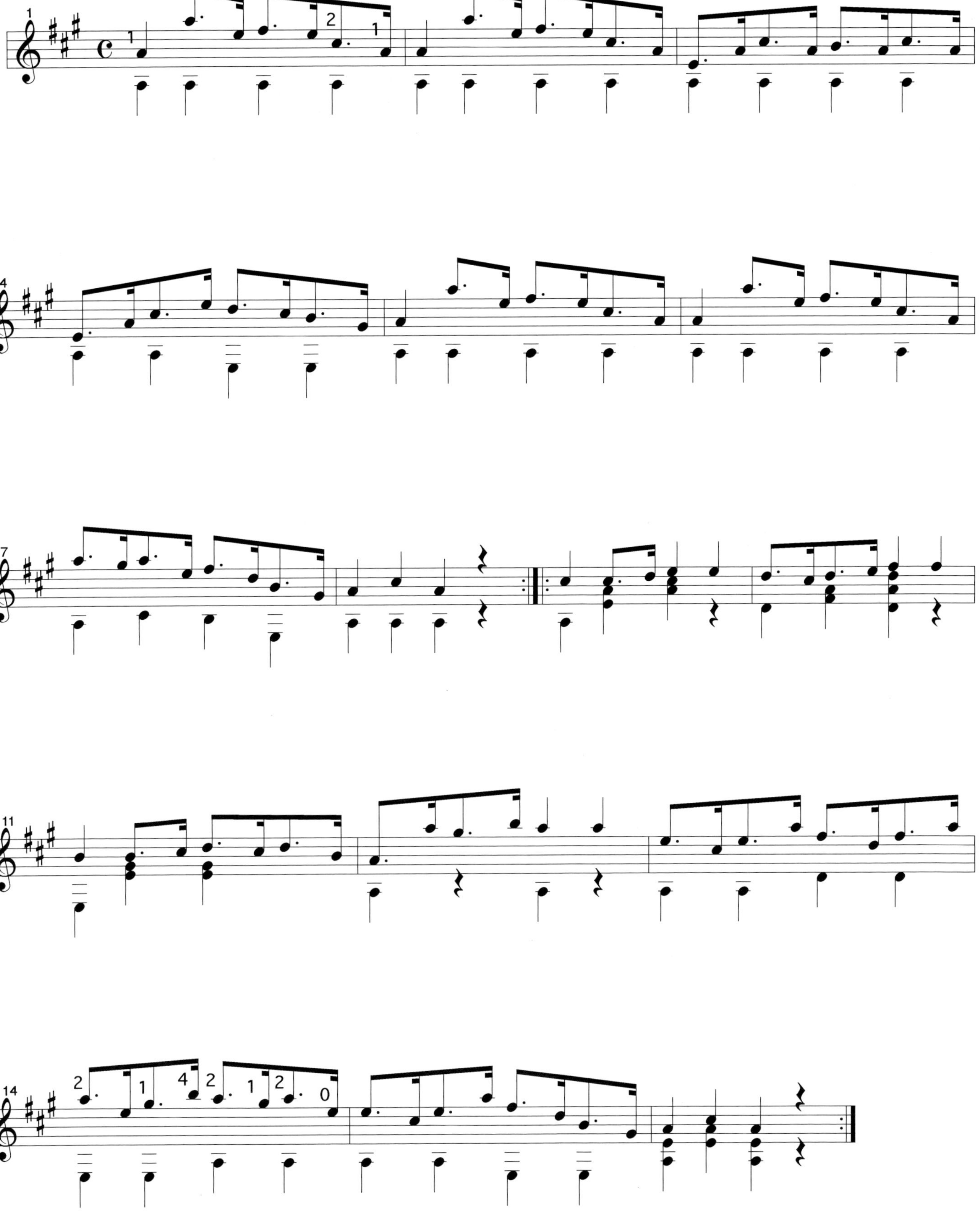

16

Highland Fling

Traditional
(arranged for guitar by Ed Munger)

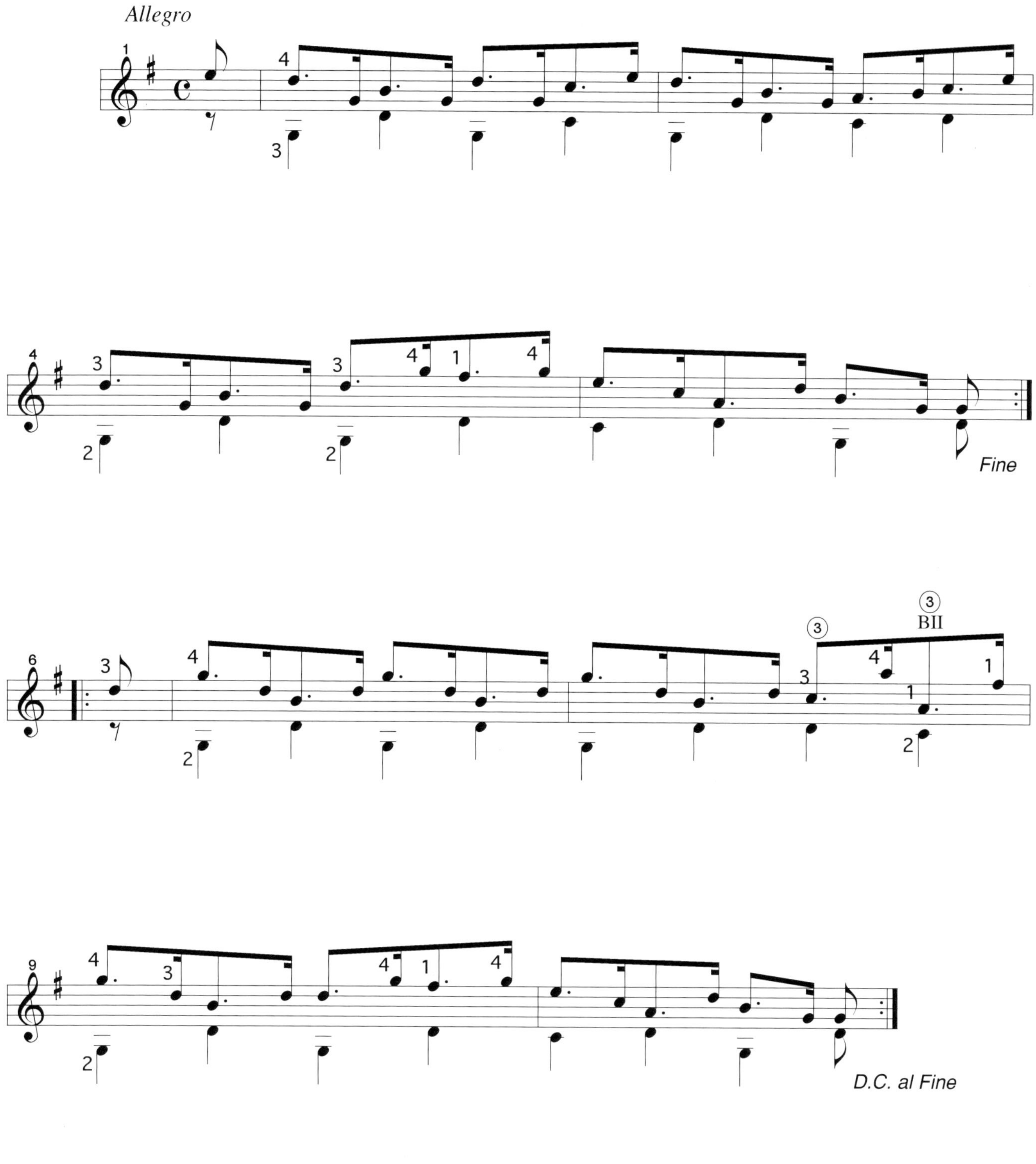

17

Roy's Wife of Aldivalloch

Highland Reel

Traditional
(arranged for guitar by Ed Munger)

6th = D
5th = G

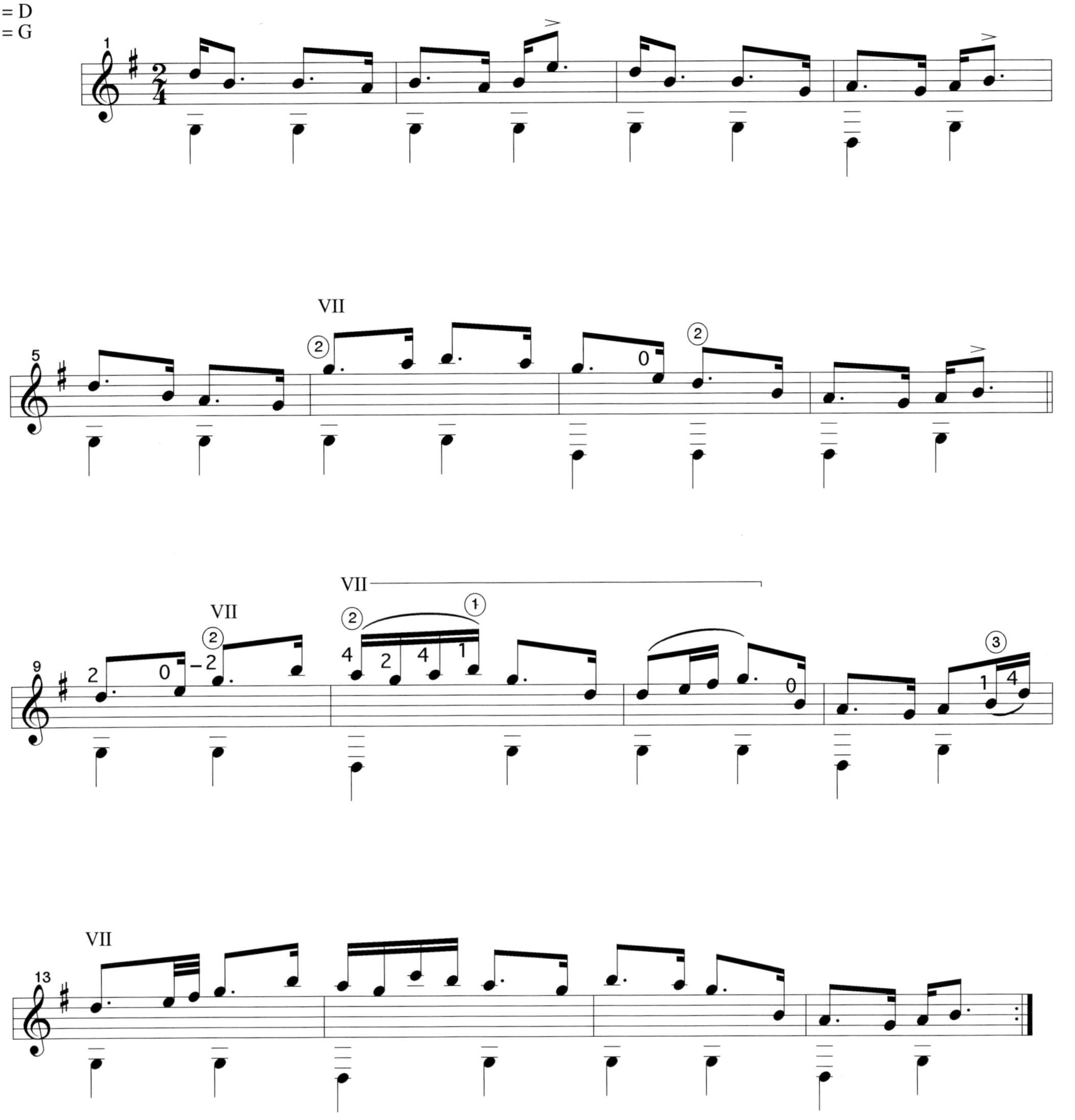

18

Rosa Lee

Malbrook
(arranged for guitar by Ed Munger)

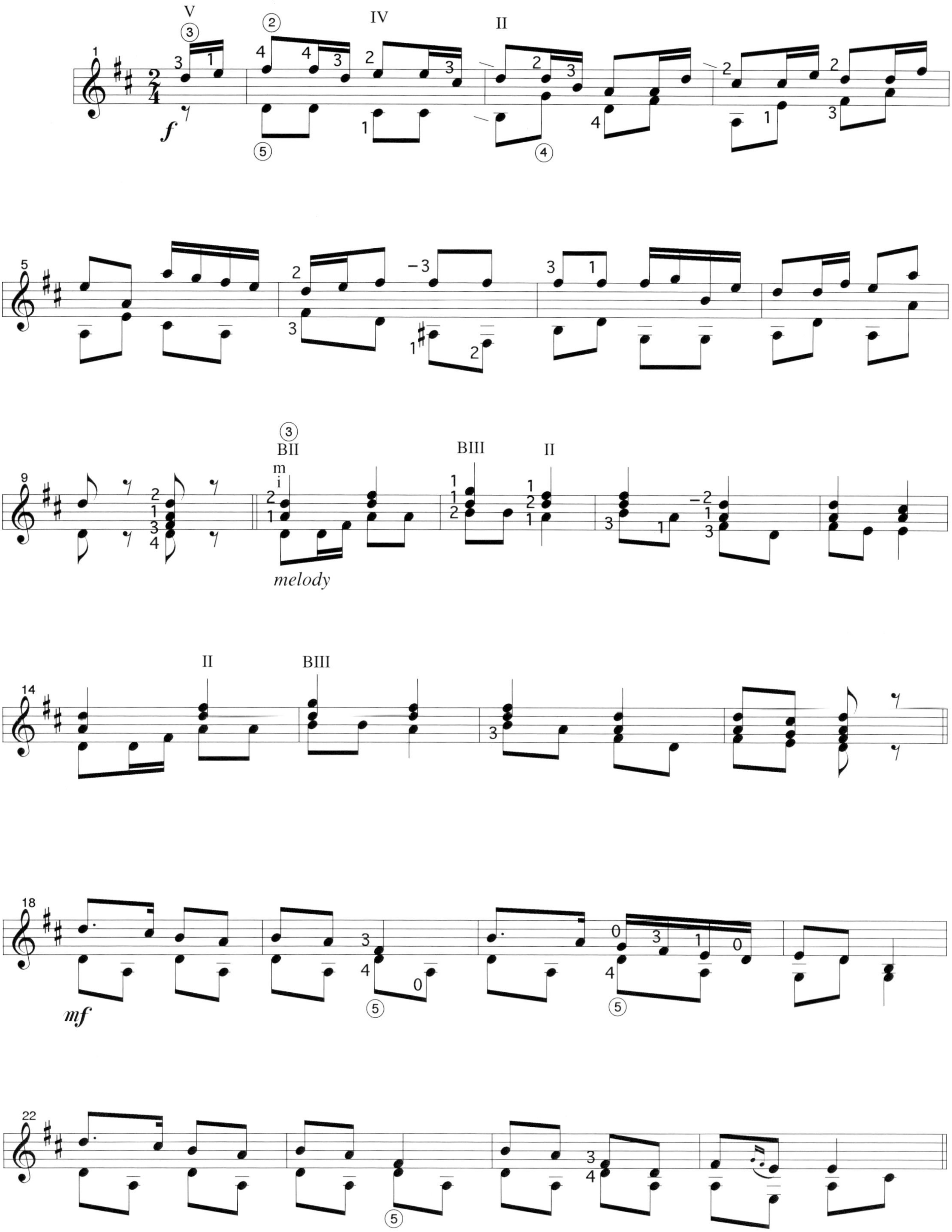

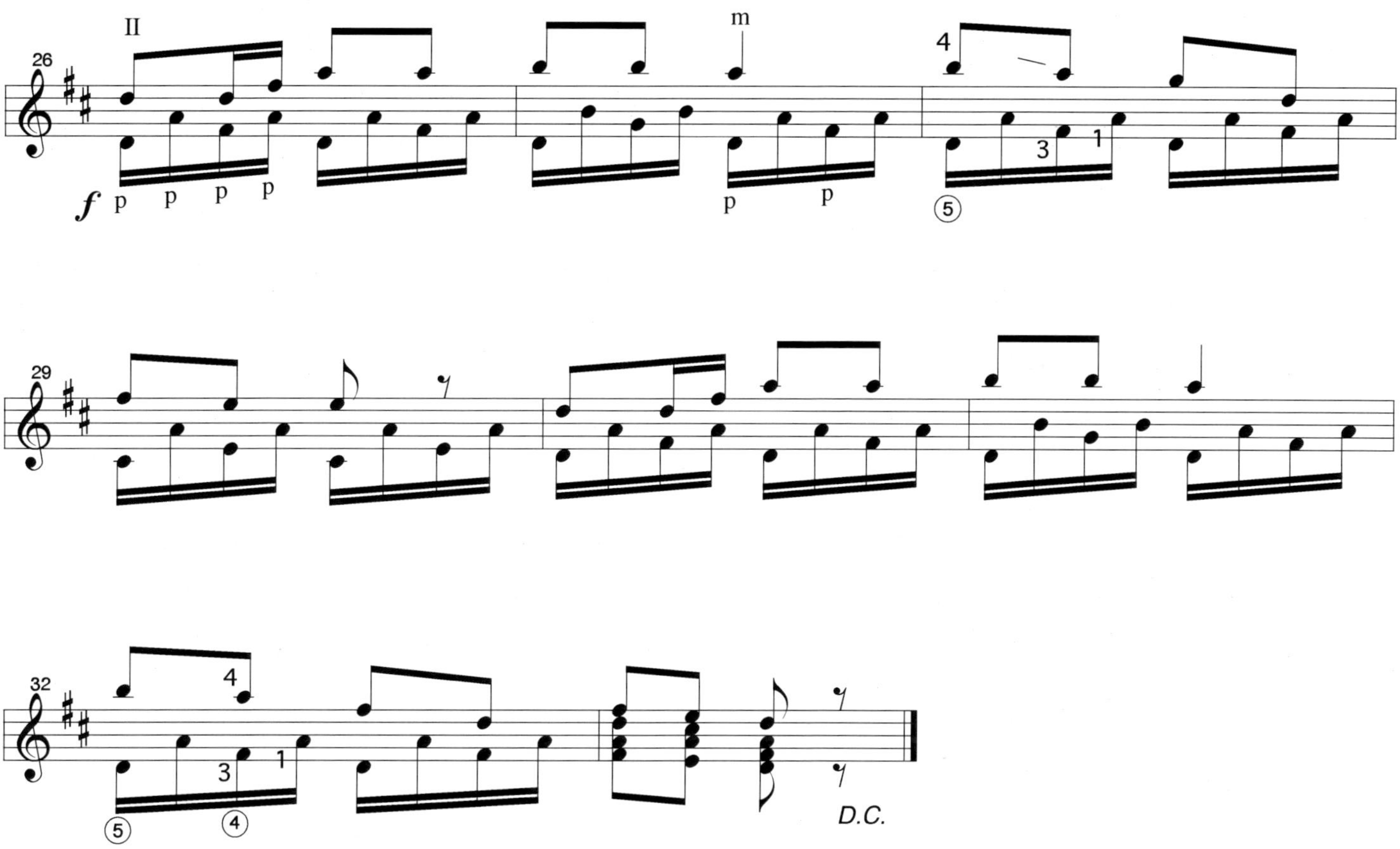
26
II
m
p p p p p p
4
3 1
⑤
29
32
4
3 1
⑤ ④
D.C.

19

Original Banjo Dance

W.K. Batchelder
(arranged for guitar by Ed Munger)

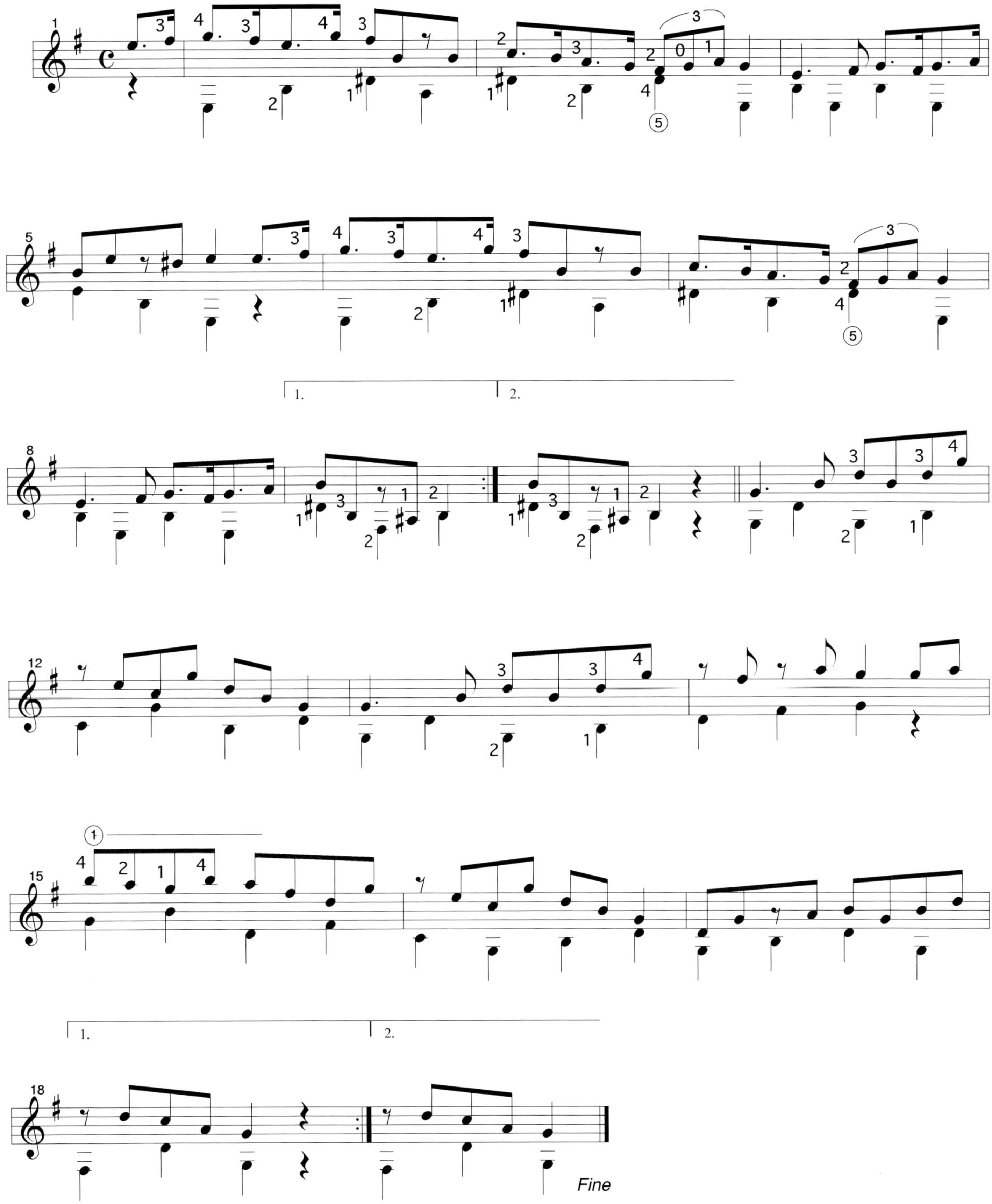

20

Kinlock

Traditional
(arranged for guitar by Ed Munger)

(original in E♭)

6th = D

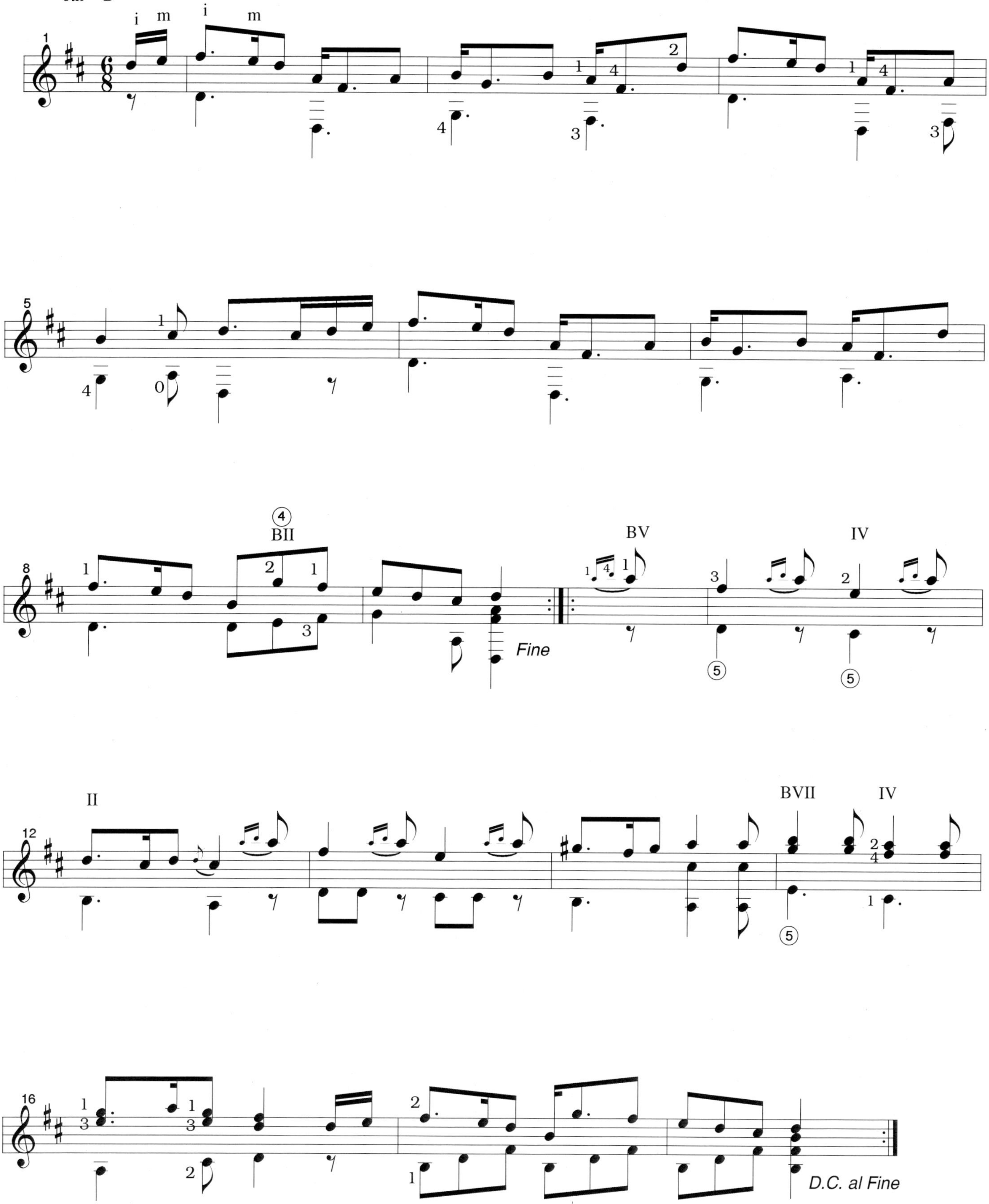

21

Speed the Plough

Traditional
(arranged for guitar by Ed Munger)

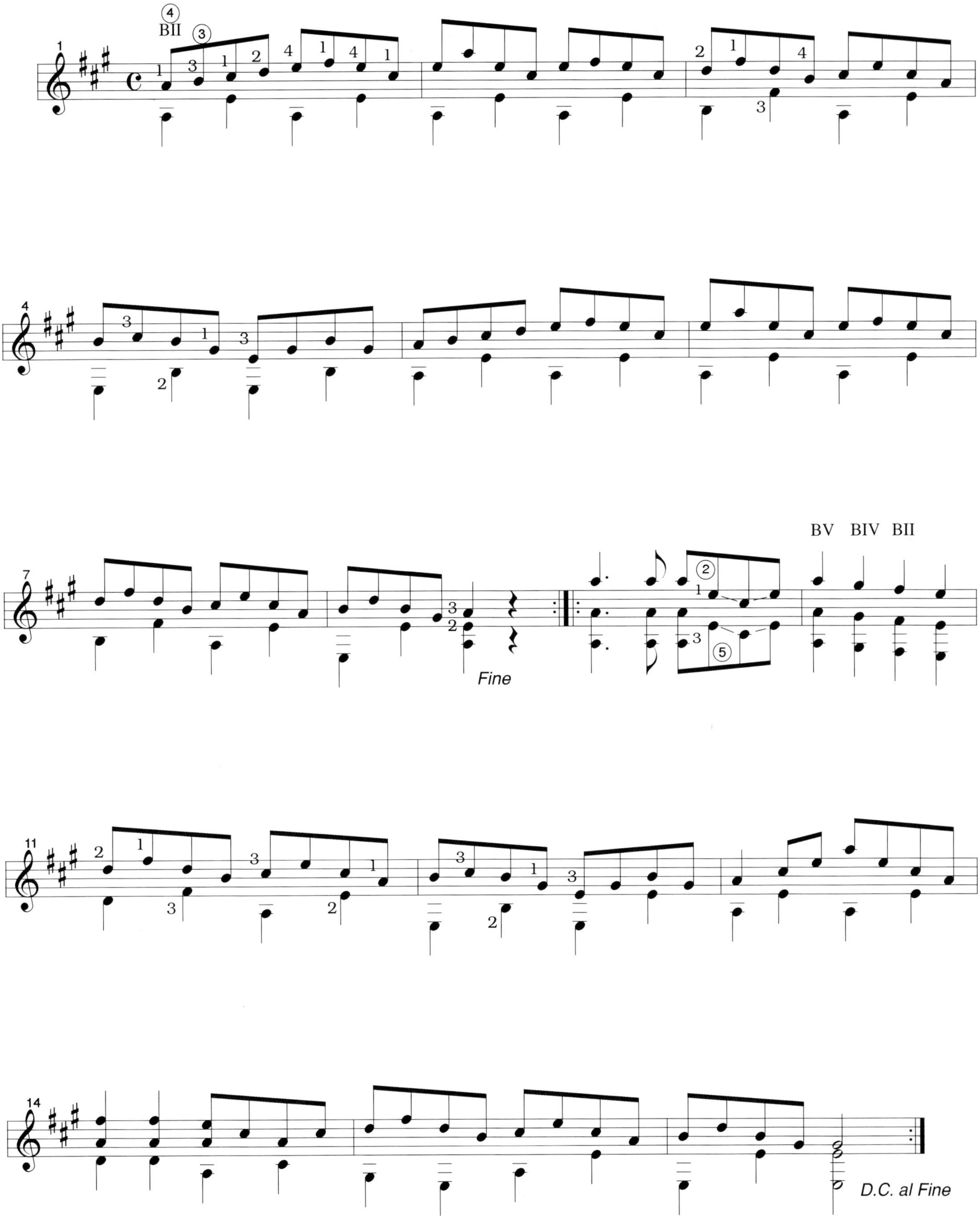

22

Miss McLeod's Reel

Traditional
(arranged for guitar by Ed Munger)

6th = D
5th = G

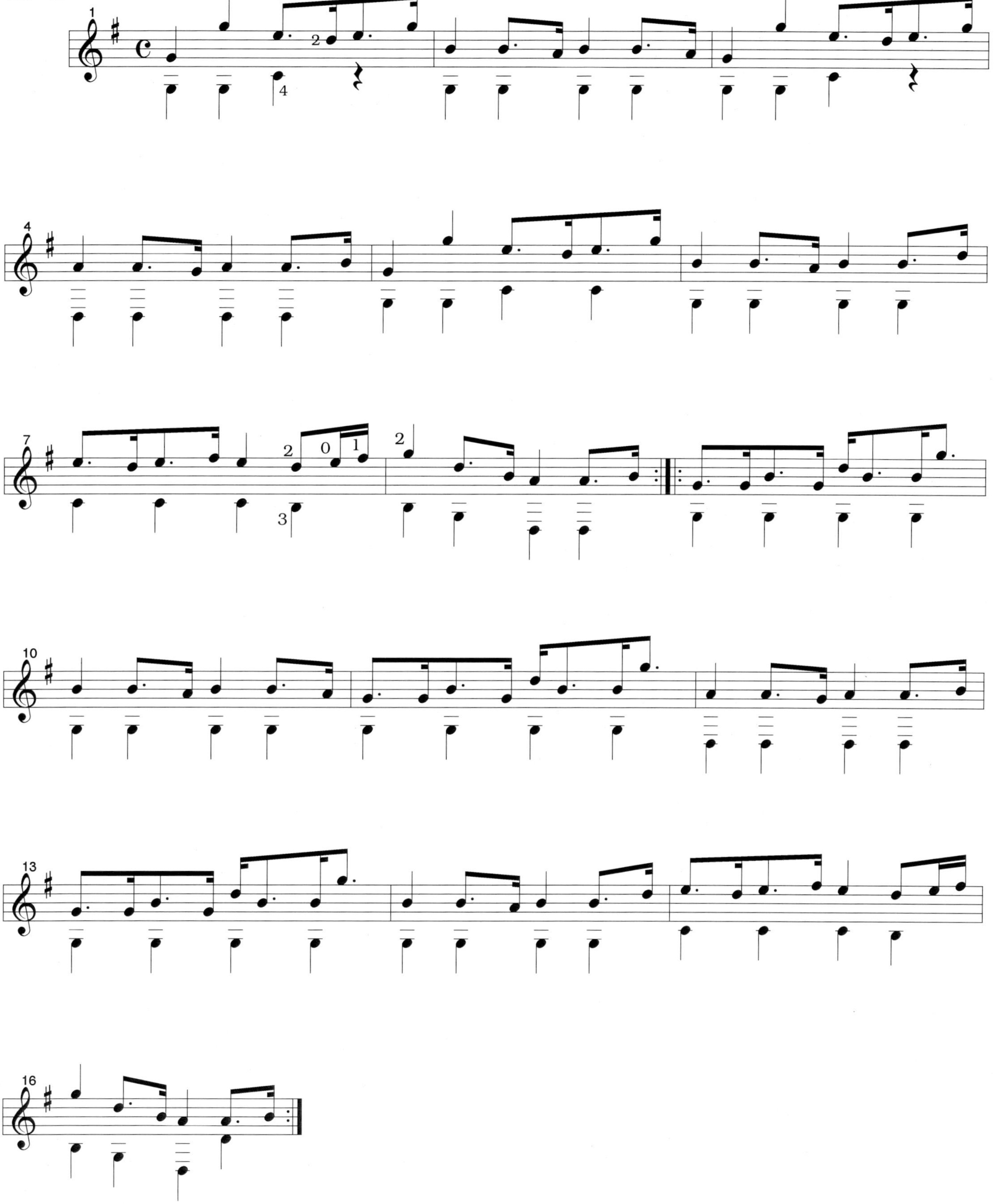

23

Martha

Traditional
(arranged for guitar by Ed Munger)

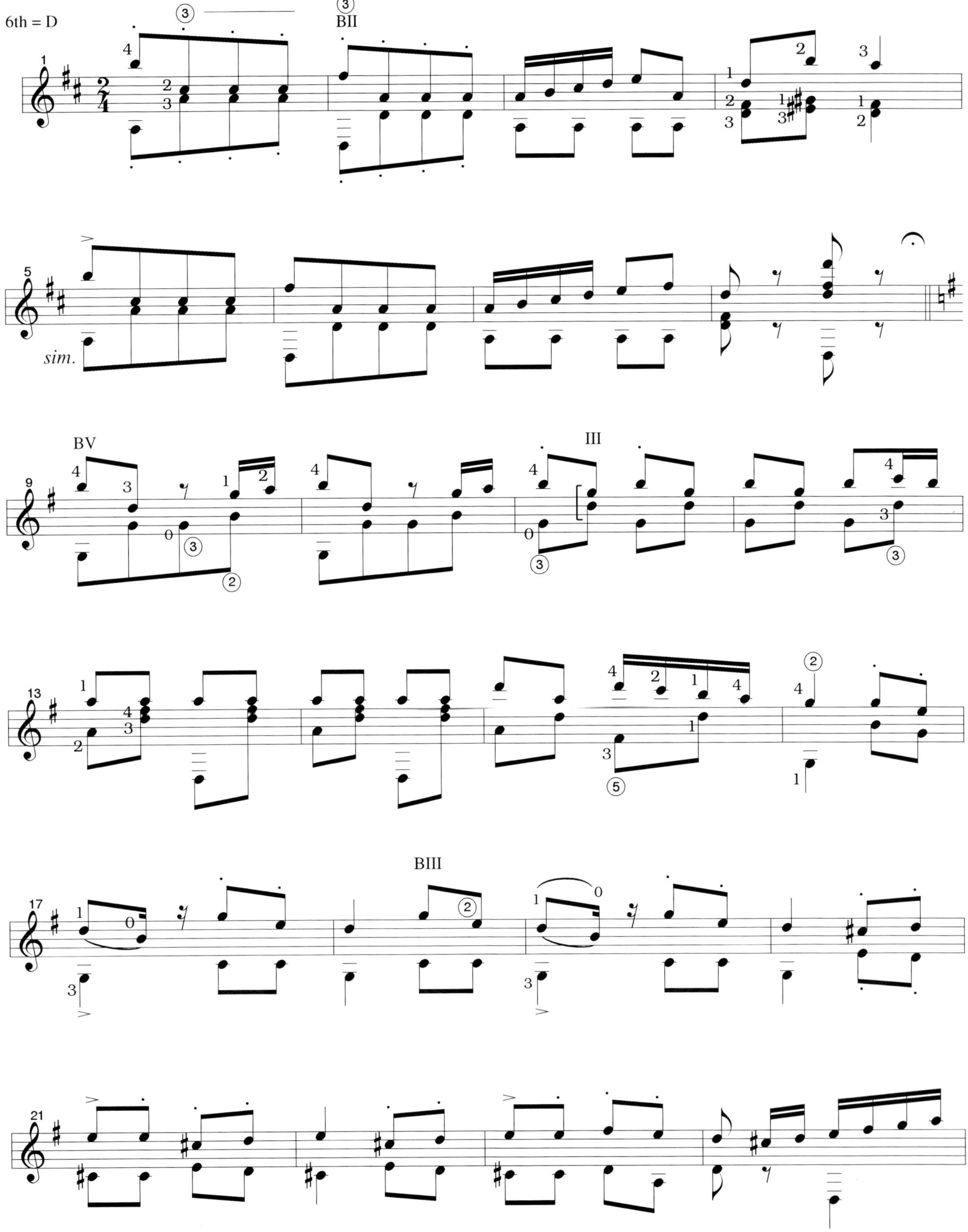

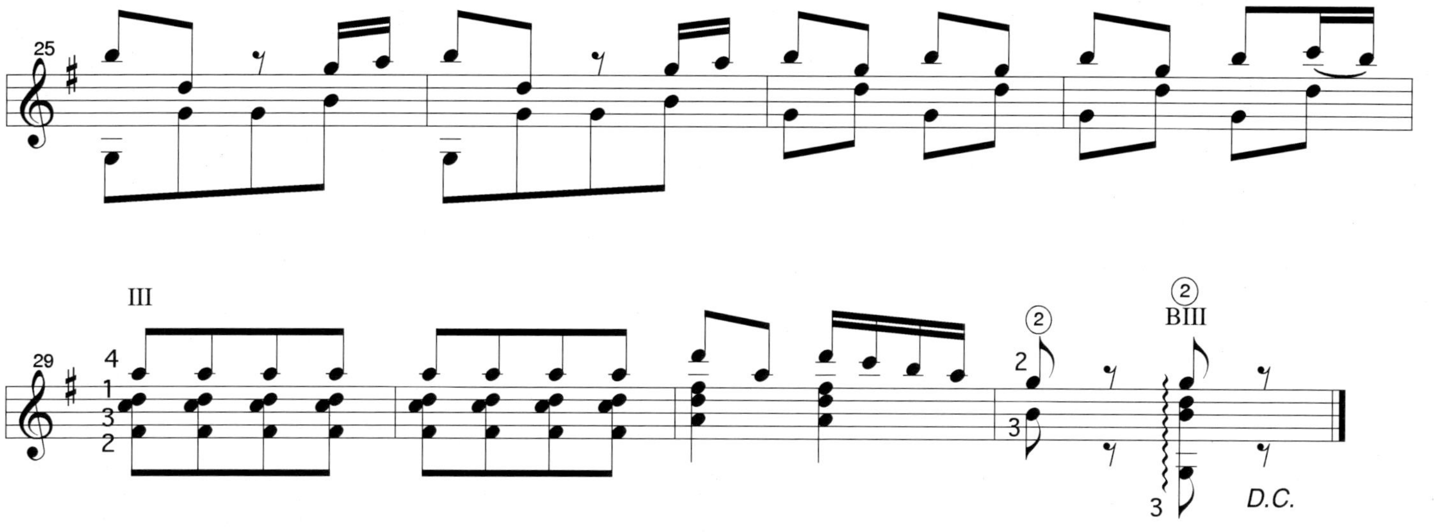
25
III
29
BIII
D.C.

24

Virginia
Lord MacDonald's Reel

B. Arlington
(arranged for guitar by Ed Munger)

Allegretto

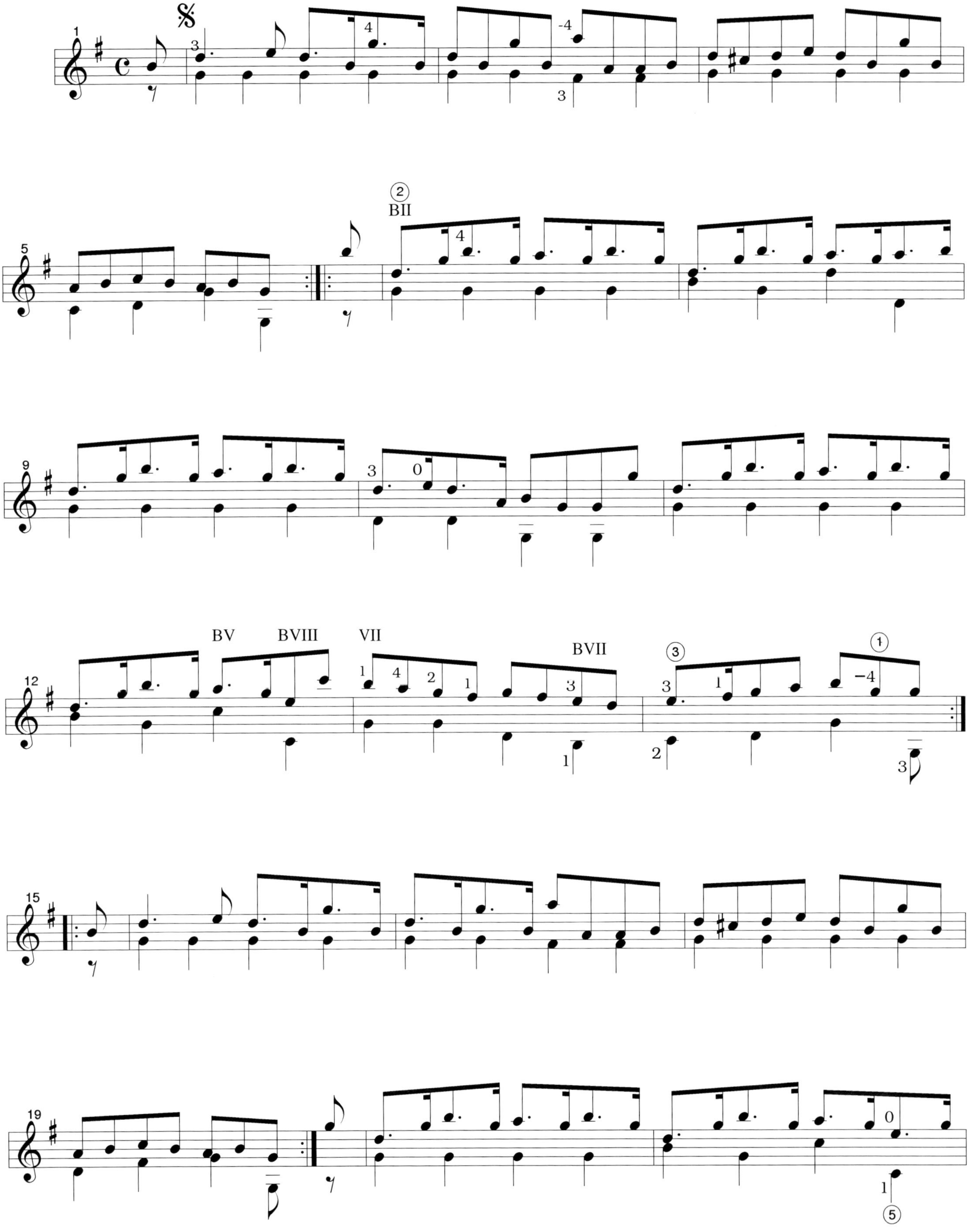

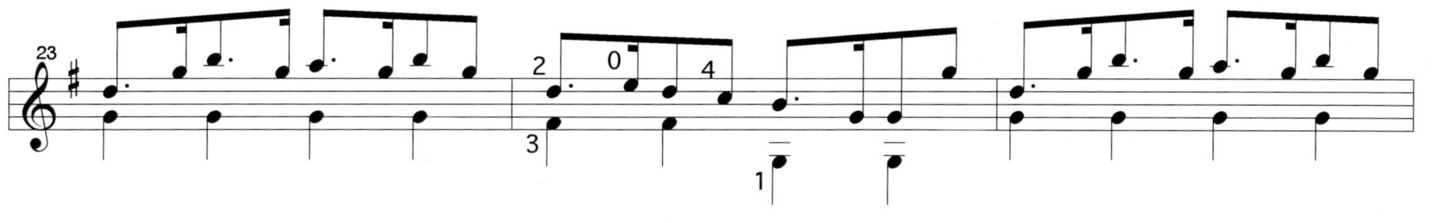
23
2
0
4
3
1

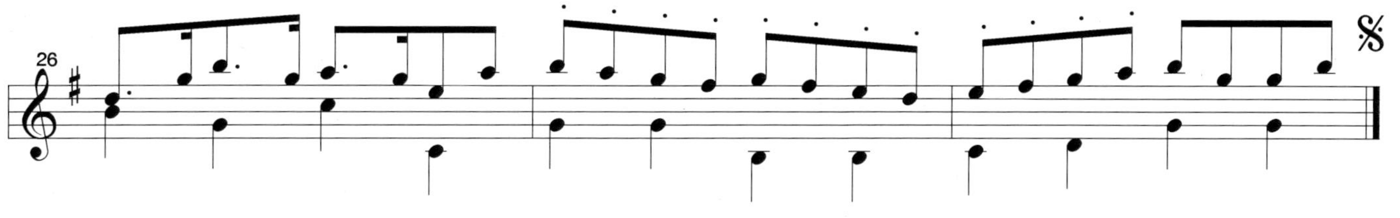
26

The Highland Lassie

B. Arlington
(arranged for guitar by Ed Munger)

(original in F)

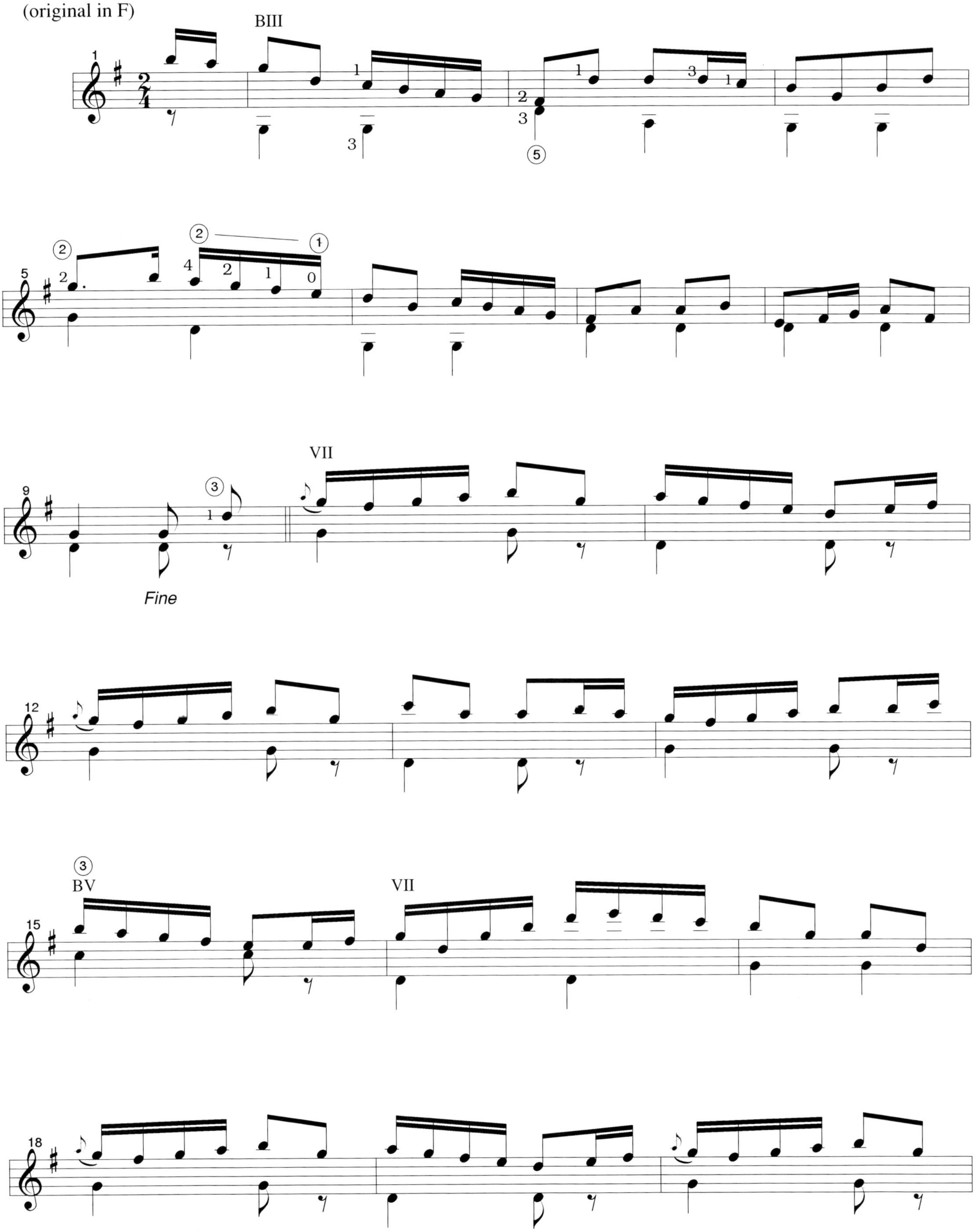

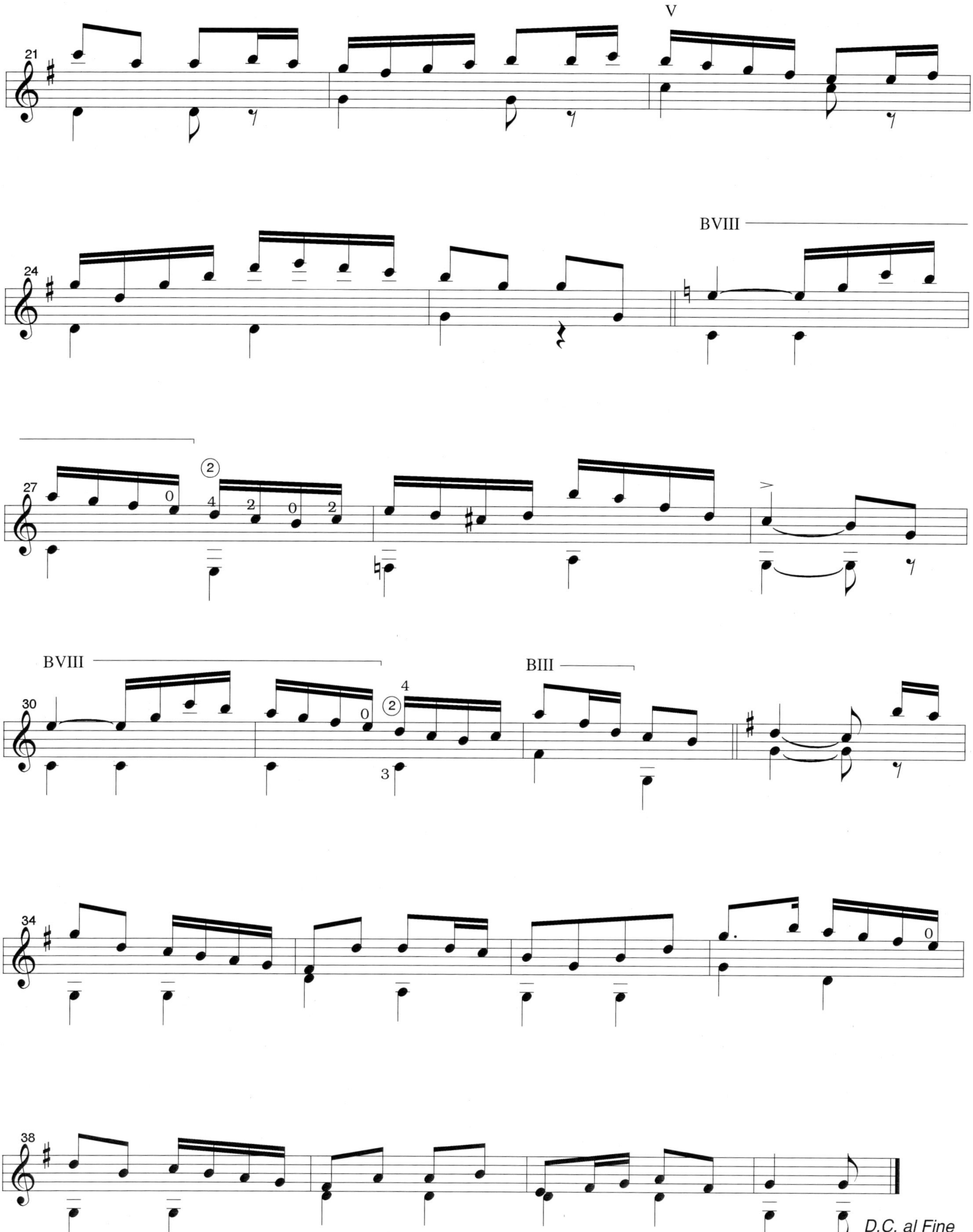
V
BVIII
BVIII
BIII
D.C. al Fine

Farewell Bonnie Scotland

B. Arlington
(arranged for guitar by Ed Munger)

(original in B♭)

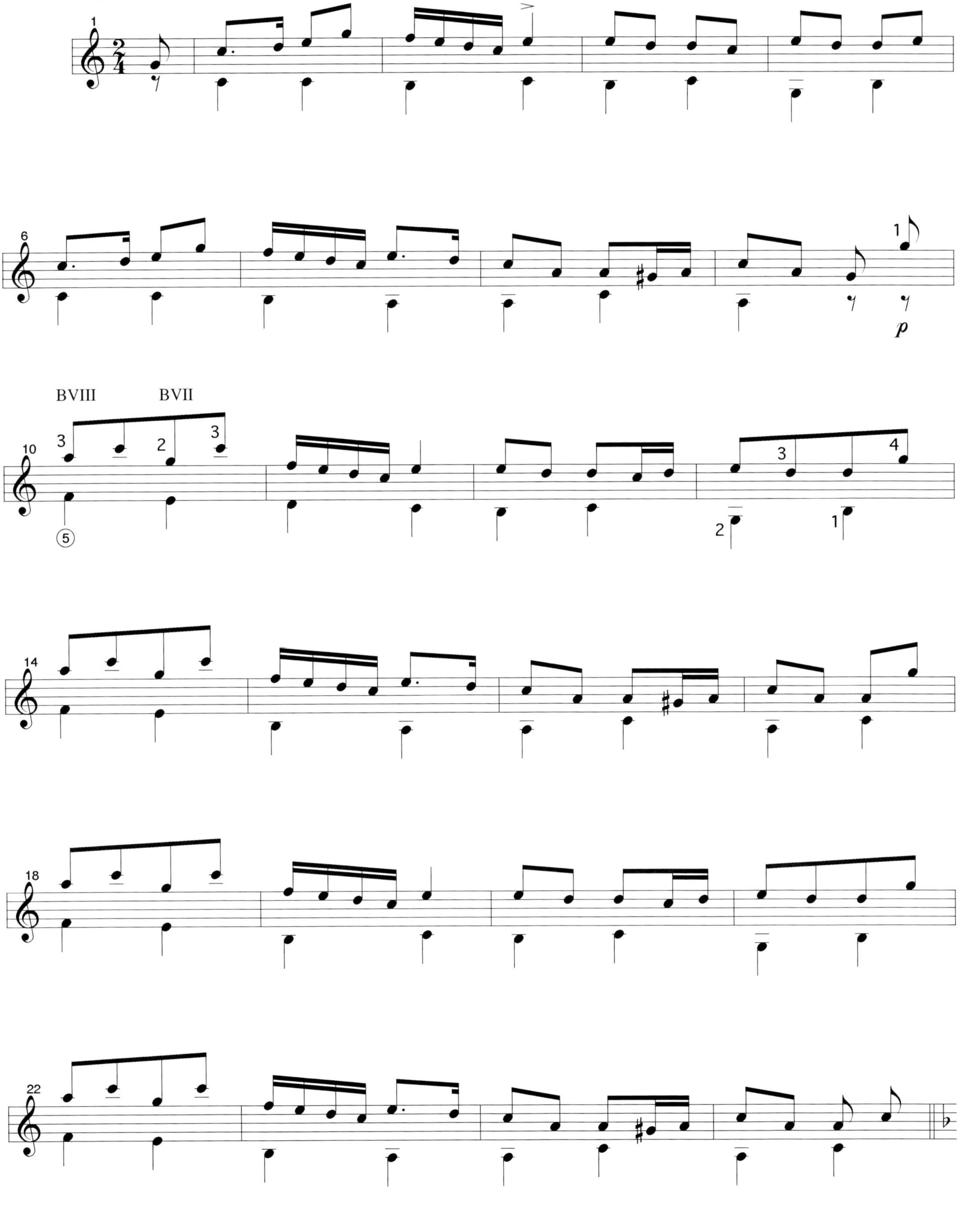

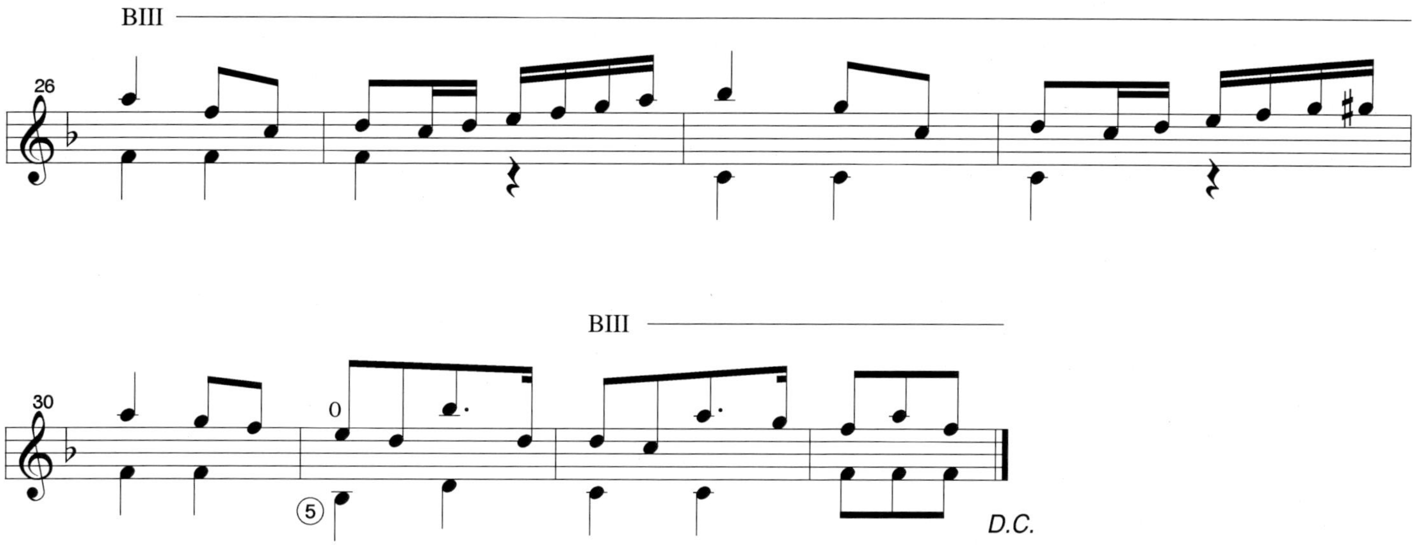
BIII
26
BIII
30
0
5
D.C.

Chorus Jig

Traditional
(arranged for guitar by Ed Munger)

5th = G

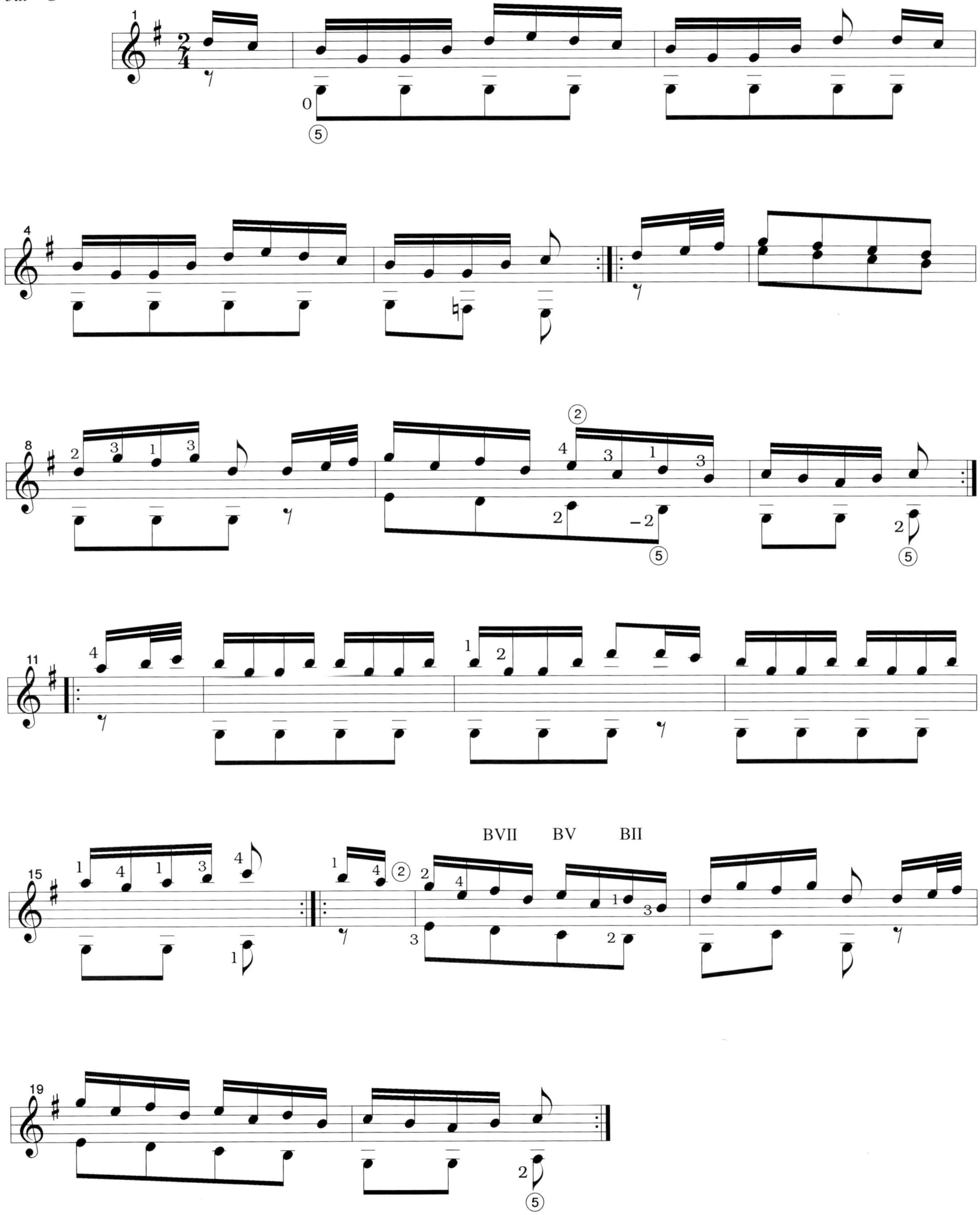

The Campbells Are Comin'

B. Arlington
(arranged for guitar by Ed Munger)

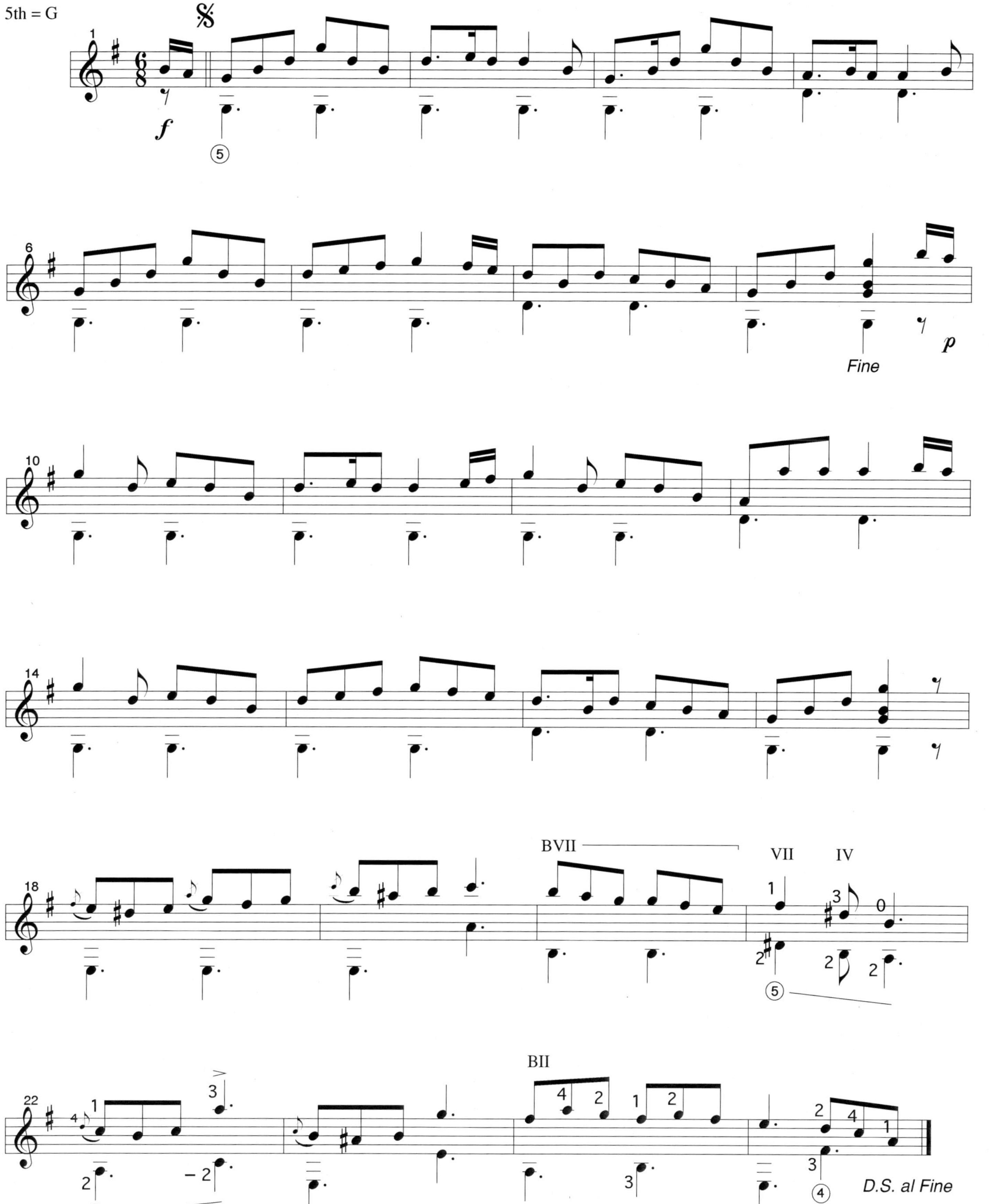

This page has been
left blank to avoid
awkward page turns

29

There's Nae Luck About The House

B. Arlington
(arranged for guitar by Ed Munger)

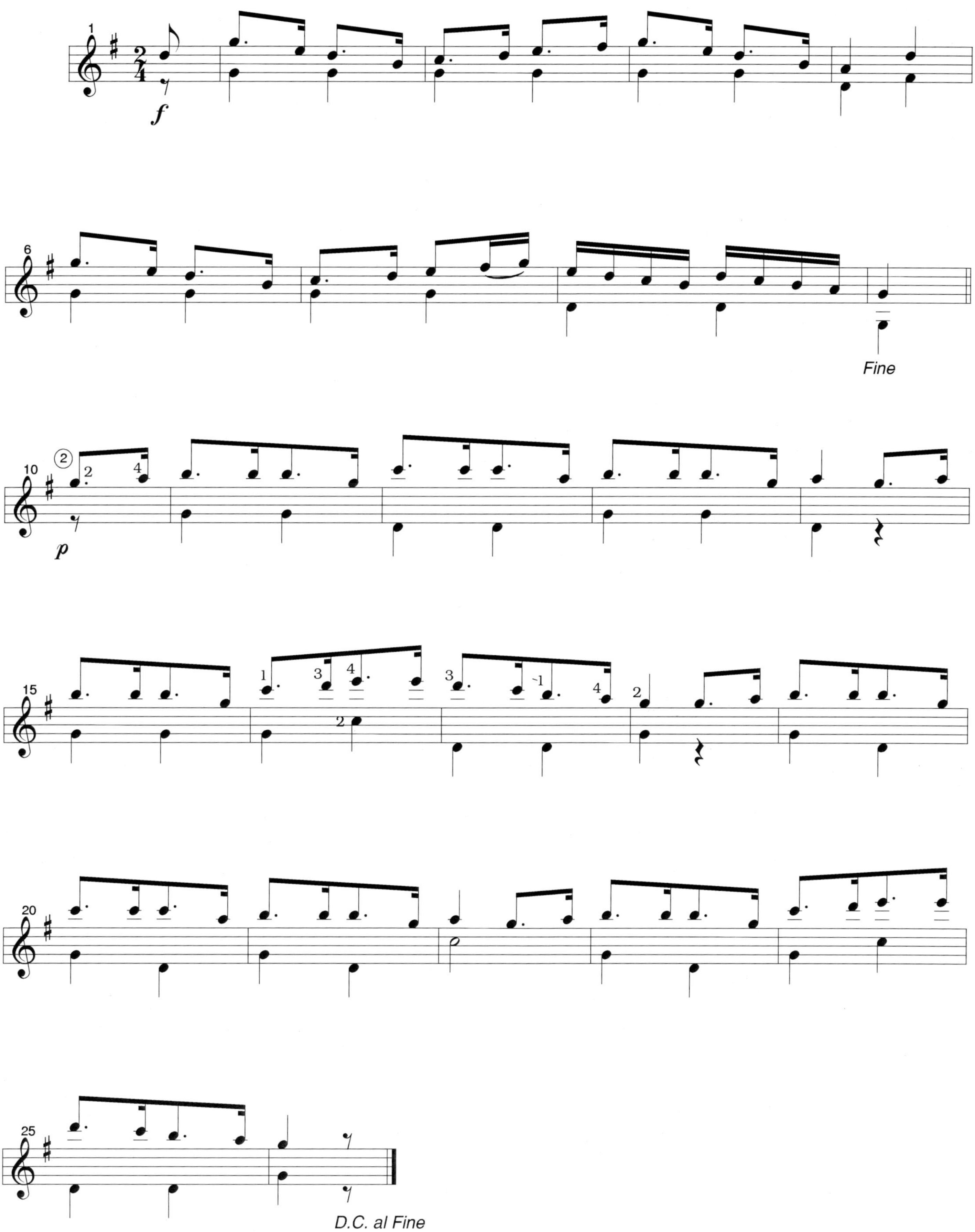

30

My Love She's But A Lassie Yet

B. Arlington
(arranged for guitar by Ed Munger)

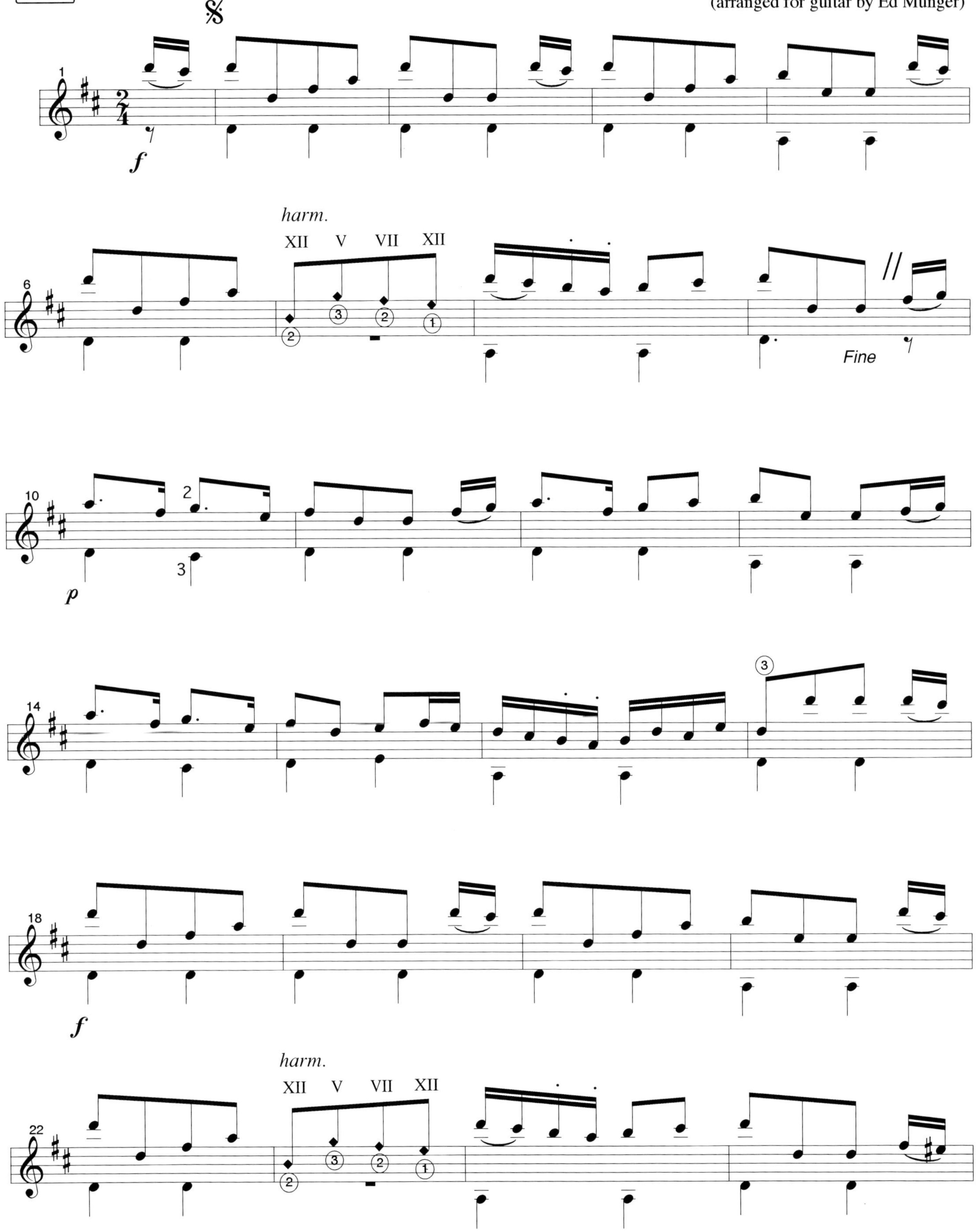

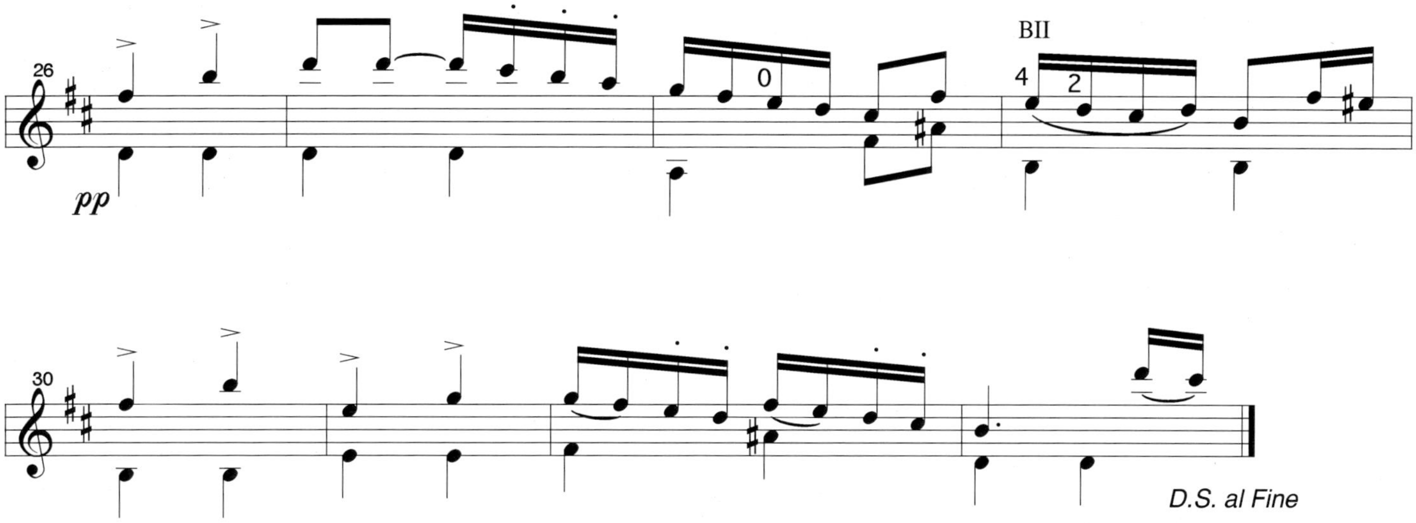

BII
pp
D.S. al Fine

About the Author

Edward W. Munger was born April 8, 1942 in Albany, New York. He started playing piano at age 5 and by 11 he was playing guitar. Edward studied Mel Bay's Modern Guitar Method, Grades 1-7.

He attended Berklee School of Music in Boston where he took a professional course in arranging as well as taking masters lessons from Jorge Morel in New York City. He was on the adjunct faculty at the College of St. Rose for Classical Guitar and offered a course for Jazz Guitar at Union College and a course for Blues Guitar at Empire College in Saratoga.

Edward played at the Saratoga Performing Arts Center, Proctors Theatre, and Colonie Stardust Theatre and is a member of Retreat House Folk Group. He is the Director of Ed Munger Music Studios where he teaches guitar and voice.

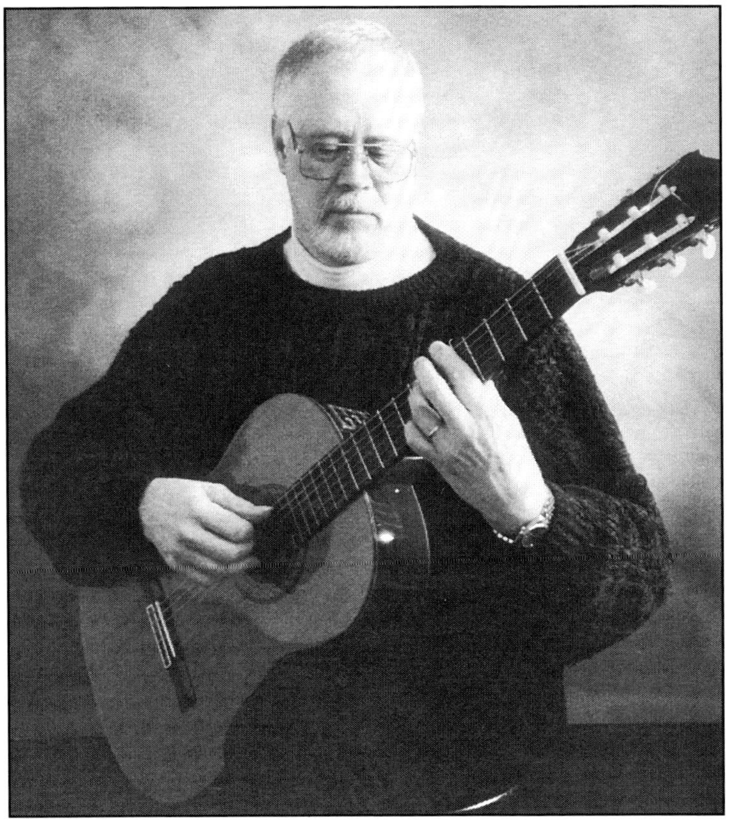